östberg™

Library of Design Management

ADVANCE PRAISE FOR

COMMUNICATION BY DESIGN

I found Joan's book to be an easy read and would recommend it
to a broad range of professionals. For those who have followed these
principles most of their professional lives, the book serves as a reminder
of things too often forgotten; for those new to the game,
it provides a checklist of things never to forget.

JOSEPH L. FLEISCHER, FAIA
Partner, Polshek Partnership Architects

Joan Capelin has developed a "must read" book for any public relations
practitioner starting his or her own consulting business or beginning any
new organizational management responsibility. Not only are her twenty-
four principles of value to those with new management and business
development needs, they are basically what every young manager "needs
to know" and what older seasoned public relations managers "should
know." Capelin is brief, to the point, insightful, on target and witty.

MELVIN L. SHARPE, APR, Fellow PRSA
Professor and Coordinator, Graduate and Undergraduate Public
Relations Programs, Ball State University

Joan Capelin's new book, *Communication by Design*, is an easy read and very
enjoyable. She has explored principles that we sometimes take for
granted and compiled them in a way that reminds us that these are the
roots of our design profession's success. As we revisit the Core Values
of Durrant, we will be making Joan's book mandatory reading
for our Leadership Group.

CHARLES R. MARSDEN, PE
President & COO, The Durrant Group, Inc.

This book got my attention. Every principal should read this book and have it on his or her desk for handy reference. So should all professionals, from the new graduate on up. Succinct, clever, and sprinkled with interesting, real-world anecdotes, it is incredibly well-written and rich with Communication by Design.

RAYMOND F. MESSER, P.E.
President and Chairman of the Board , Walter P. Moore

Joan Capelin has an excellent gift for writing. *Communication by Design* is a fast read, it is uplifting, entertaining, positive and it's brimming over with intelligent advice, presented with wit and humor. This is a refreshing "must read" for all principals, whose responsibilities include winning new work and keeping it, one of the most important components for success; it should be in the library of all principals in the design and construction industry.

JOAN GERNER
Senior Vice President, Bovis Lend Lease LMB, Inc.

I found Communication by Design a very informative and enjoyable read. I would recommend the book to a number of people who should not only read your principles but take them to heart and make sure that many are implemented. The short case study approach brings these ideas to life. These "tales from real life" leap off the page and land squarely in our sometimes-too-busy principals' lives. You have provided our industry a valuable "text book" that is really not a text book at all, not in its style, candor or richness of experience. It is rather a look into our work lives and how we can improve and enjoy that life.

JOSEPH E. BROWN, FASLA
President/CEO, EDAW

COMMUNICATION

BY DESIGN

MARKETING PROFESSIONAL SERVICES

COMMUNICATION

BY DESIGN

MARKETING PROFESSIONAL SERVICES

JOAN CAPELIN

FOREWORD BY WELD COXE
FOREWORD BY C. E. VICK, JR.

Greenway Communications   **östberg**

Significant portions of this book by Joan Capelin were originally published under the title, Principles for Principals and published by SMPS.

Cover Design by Austin Cramer
Layout by Jennie Monahan

Östberg Library of Design Management

ISBN: 0-9675477-4-1

Library of Congress Cataloging-in-Publication Data

Greenway Communications, LLC
a division of The Greenway Group, Inc.
30 Technology Parkway South, Suite 200
Atlanta, GA 30092
(800) 726-8603
www.greenway.us

For the two most important men in my life

Stanley J. Capelin, my very special father and pioneering management consultant
Your principles made life easier and more rewarding for thousands of people. Your handshake—such big hands!—calmed clients and friends and made them feel protected. You gave me my first job in public relations the summer I was sixteen, launching my professional career, even though—how well I recall—you felt that women should not work. I wish you could be here to read this book.

David Paul Helpern, my superb husband and excellent architect
There is no one better, kinder, or more supportive. You were the first architect I ever met, and through you, I have seen such beautiful places and discovered how I could best serve others.

CONTENTS

ACKNOWLEDGMENTS

In a company where process is so critical and the pace is rapid, we have a rule (not a principle): Don't go into Joan's office without a pad and pencil in hand—to receive instructions, a request, or language. By the same token, I compulsively run a to-do list. That's how things get done around here.

As this book went into preparation, I was the one walking around with a notepad, so I could remember all the people who helped me. It's amazing how much help I needed and received.

First, let me thank the staff of Capelin Communications. Liz Battista did the heavy lifting with exceptional grace and skill. Without her, there would be no book. Caroline Miller Wolfe was the first person in the office to urge me on, and she was my first editor. Michael Singer took things off my desk as fast as he could, so I could work on the book. Judy Rowe especially knows that it was not easy keeping me on a publishing schedule while we were trying to run a business and keep the clients happy.

For the first edition, *Communication by Design* was titled *Principles for Principals: Insights and Anecdotes about What Makes Professional Service Firms Thrive.* That title was published as a special run by the Society for Marketing Professional Services, an association I have supported since its founding. Executive Director Ron Worth, Communications Director Lisa Jenkins Bowman, and Bookstore Manager Melanie Doon were enthusiastic and professional participants.

Publishing a book is challenging. As Jim Cramer said to me when he gave the book its second life, "real" name, and new look, "Nothing sells itself" (how's that for a principle!). I have known and admired Jim for probably 20 years and am truly pleased that I could expand and transfer the manuscript to his excellent Ostberg team.

I innocently asked Jane Weishaus, who has spent a career in publishing, if the principles and anecdotes would be clear to readers outside the design and construction world. The two weeks that she scrutinized each page and graciously advised us were exhilarating. Every page has something of Jane on it.

Weld Coxe began marketing for the professional services and then founded The Coxe Group to help an awakening industry. He was an early client of mine and a constant booster, as I became more of a presence in the industry—there is no more valuable or better supporter than he. I am understandably proud that this iconic figure has written one of the forewords for me.

I had admired C. E. ("Ed") Vick, Jr. for the way he founded and grew Kimley-Horn & Associates, Inc. Then I got to know him well while working with him on the board of PSMA the year he was its president. This fine gentleman broke into his family holiday to write his foreword. Ed said, "As usual, you make me look good." *Au contraire*, Ed: You honor me.

I asked an enormous squad of people to review the book. Some of them also scrutinized each page and gave me their comments, so that the book would be coherent and powerful. Their eyes greatly complemented those of the professional proofreader. These colleagues included Lee Benish, Friedrich Bohm, Joe Brown, Joe Fleischer, Jim Franklin, Joan Gerner, Gary Gordon, Faye Harwell, Robert Ivy, Norman Koonce, F. M. "Chunky" Latham, Charlie Marsden, Ray Messer, Peter Piven, Al Potter, Mel Sharpe, Lee Waldron, Richard

Behind every author there has got to be an astute legal adviser. David Ebert really knows his stuff.

Robert Rich, Roz Burak, and Dr. Joanne Intrator held my hand—and sometimes held it to the fire. They are very smart people, and I was well advised to listen to them.

David Helpern and our daughter, Lauren Helpern, have been wise and vigilant advisers. Plus, David designed the most wonderful, elegant home office for me, and then brought home dinner most nights for the two years that this effort has taken. How lucky can you be?

It's been an amazing journey—a privilege to work with the complex, imaginative, resilient, brilliantly educated people who design and build on this planet, many of whom appear on these pages, many of them named. I've been asked why I haven't taken my communications skills elsewhere. Why ever would I? I get to spend my time with the people who dream and then shape the future.

FOREWORD

Weld Coxe

J oan Capelin is one of that handful of professionals in the management and marketing of design and construction firms of whom it can be said: "Been there, done that!" Therefore, any time Joan shares from her reservoir of experience, it is well worth the read.

In this volume, Joan shares principles that shape and guide her view of management and of marketing communications. Best of all, she illustrates her principles with many anecdotes that give credibility to the points. Her objective can be summed up in two excerpts from the text:

"No matter what people say, what they really want to achieve is to get more work."

"People want something that works for them, to get them going in the right direction."

That said, no one in the trenches of managing or marketing professional design or construction services could read Joan's principles without being tempted to share his/her own. This is one of Joan's very points: There is no one list of principles. The goal is to have some core principles and know what they are.

Here are mine.

It's all about projects. The client has little or no interest in your marketing plan or communication strategy or personnel problems or etc. The client has a project to be done and wants above all else to believe you want to give it your total professional attention.

Marketers who get caught up in *getting* the project can miss the point that no one in the firm may want to *do* it. As Eugene Kohn once asked: "Do we just want the job? Or do we want the opportunity to do it?" Any firm that gets confused or is in conflict over this will have trouble projecting a winning attitude to clients, prospective clients, or its staff.

The role of Management in a design firm is to keep the firm from getting in the way of projects. The role of Leadership is to be sure the entire organization knows the difference. Too often we get caught up in what seem to be the priorities of the organization and divert the attention of staff into tasks of management. As soon as marketing encounters resistance to its priorities, for instance, it is time to remind ourselves what professional practice is about, and that is projects, projects, projects. The best interest of the smallest project in the office should always come first.

The bottom line is rarely the bottom line in a successful design firm. It is important for a firm to be *businesslike*, but the minute it shifts its emphasis to being a business, rather than being primarily about design and delivery of projects, it will inevitably falter in the marketplace. The client wants to know you care about his/her project before you care about your pocketbook.

I know there may be readers who will disagree with some of my principles, but that is the point of Joan's contribution to the literature. As the functions of management and marketing in a professional design firm have evolved over the past generation, we are constantly learning new approaches to getting and doing projects. Each firm must eventually decide by what principles it will operate day to day.

Joan Capelin has contributed a fresh book to the marketing and management shelf of your library. Her point is: It is important to choose the principles that will guide you and your organization. The menu is long, yet if you enjoy the challenge of finding your own compass, the rewards will include your own collection of anecdotes.

Read on.

Weld Coxe
Block Island, Rhode Island
January 2004

Weld Coxe, FSMPS, Hon. AIA, is the emeritus founding principal of The Coxe Group, an internationally prominent management consulting firm serving the design and construction industry. He is a Distinguished Visiting Professor at the School of Architecture of Rensselaer Polytechnic Institute, has taught at the University of Pennsylvania, and at the Harvard Graduate School of Design. From 1990 to 1993, Mr. Coxe co-chaired an International Union of Architects work group researching world trends in private practice in twenty countries. He has authored three books.

FOREWORD

C.E. ("Ed") Vick, Jr.

It is a distinct pleasure for me to write a foreword for Joan Capelin. I can think of no person more capable of writing this book. She has provided excellent advice to principals of design and construction firms for many years. I have personally benefited from her excellent advice about how to communicate well.

All principals should take advantage of this type of professional advice; it is most valuable. For instance, I experienced a measure of triumph when a senior reporter of a major newspaper congratulated me on being the "best" he had ever interviewed—"best" that is, at avoiding answers to questions that I did not want to answer, yet still giving him credible information for his story. This compliment was a direct result of coaching by a public relations professional. I am a believer!

It is most important for principals to establish "core values" for their firms based upon principles given in this book. The first-generation owners of our firm (Kimley-Horn and Associates, Inc.) did not write theirs down; they just practiced them on a daily basis. I was very proud when our second-generation owners decided to record and publish their core values for the benefit of all employees of the firm. These values were the exact same ones practiced each day by the founders. If you have not written down the core values of your firm, do it today!

In a Professional Services Management Association seminar, Weld Coxe, with whom I share the honor of writing a foreword, taught our first-generation owners that we were a "business-based practice" rather than a "practice-based business." He defined this as a firm where business is a means of earning a living, and practice is a way of living. We were proud of being a "business-based practice." And our principles, like many set forth in this book, helped us—and could help you—have a successful business.

I have always said, "A professional service firm has no reason to exist other than to serve clients." Always require exceptional client service in your organization. Other principles that guided the development and achievements of Kimley-Horn, many of which are found in this book, include:

Surround yourself with "10s."

Always hire professionals who are smarter than you.

Hire self-starters and get out of their way.

Have high expectations. Set goals and measure progress against these goals.

Share the wealth. Good people are motivated by money. It is honorable to make money and thrive financially.

Grow with the soul of a small company.

Do not have profit centers. Share one pot of money at the end of the year.

Provide an environment in which your employees can flourish in all aspects of life.

Joan has given you good, sound advice in this book. Read and follow it to obtain greater success in your business enterprise!

C.E. ("Ed") Vick Jr.
Raleigh, North Carolina
February 2004

Vick is a founder of Kimley-Horn and Associates, Inc., a Raleigh-based engineering, planning, and environmental consulting firm of over 1,300 employees. He is a Fellow of the Institute of Transportation Engineers, a Fellow of the American Society of Civil Engineers, and member of the American Institute of Certified Planners. He has frequently served as adviser to the North Carolina State University Kenan Institute for Engineering, Technology & Science. Mr. Vick is now Kimley-Horn's retired chairman and remains active in his community.

INTRODUCTION

Make it happen

Principals and industry leaders of all ages want to communicate well, advocate compellingly, support their people effectively, and win every opportunity. Few, however, have ever had the chance to learn how to do this before finding themselves thrust into a position of responsibility in their field.

In my work as a public relations and marketing consultant and executive coach, over a career now of decades, I have been privileged to meet and work with the most gifted design and construction professionals: architects and designers of all stripes, consulting engineers, project managers, educators, journalists, association executives, the professionals who support the industry—the full gamut. They have shown me their view of the world as they see it today, and their vision of the new world they are designing and building, for tomorrow.

I have observed that, while most principals find their way with ease through the requirements and challenges of their discipline, many—even the true giants in their field—feel inadequate when they have to navigate and communicate outside of a familiar arena. How can they convey the benefit of their art, their vision, their talent beyond the very specific boundaries and vocabulary of design? What *else* must they know? And how can they be equally brilliant with that "everything else"?

This book is about that "everything else." I have written *Communication by Design* to ease the way for those already in leadership positions as well as those who aspire to that rank. And, while specifically addressed to the design and building community, I have written with all professional service firms very much in mind.

It is imperative for these gifted professionals to realize what they know, *and what they need to know,* beyond what their specific education and training have given them. If they are to lead successfully, they need to move fluidly both within and outside of the world of design; they need to harness and apply other skills and knowledge; and they need to operate and communicate powerfully in many worlds.

The principles in this book are meant to support that mission. Furthermore, those in leadership positions can be well served by learning how to compress their experiences into principles and anecdotes of their own. This skill will help remove at least some of the roadblocks that may hinder the achievement of their goals for themselves and for society.

How have I come to feel this strongly about professional service firms? When I was a teenager, I worked for a management consultant (my father); later, for an architect (my husband); and then, for many years, for HLW, one of the great and enduring design firms, where, it can be argued, Michael Maas and I started the first permanent marketing department in the design professions.

In 1981 I launched my own office, daring to provide public relations and marketing communications counsel for professional service firms. It wasn't—and still isn't—for the faint at heart. Yet it was something I had to do; risk wasn't even part of the equation.

My mission was to inspire and guide an entire industry and all the professions related to it, by enabling each member or entity to find its own voice. I was also bent on developing and disseminating as much information as possible about how to communicate the value of professional services. If the first rule of marketing is to find out whether there is a need for your services, then I was right on cue.

In 1988, for instance, I had the privilege of addressing a very alert, slightly anxious breakfast audience of architects and designers at the American Institute of Architects' annual convention. Why "anxious"? Because the long-awaited results of a survey about the marketing practices of AIA members were about to become public. (I had been part of the survey team and had been invited by the Institute to deliver the news.) It was a pivotal moment; some people in the room clearly wanted to kill the messenger. I remember one man put his head on the table and covered it with his hands, as if to shield himself from a nuclear attack. But the immutable news was that marketing—like it or not—had become an integral part of professional practice.

Today, many professional service firms, with characteristic optimism, continue their great effort to become businesslike in their affairs, including their marketing. The good news is that many organizations offer training and mentoring in management and marketing, and, of course, there are now consultants and high-tech tools to support these activities. The other news (notice I didn't say the "bad" news) is that, just as building a new highway to overcome traffic problems only brings more cars onto the road, competition has become as sharp as a samurai sword.

After reading *Communication by Design* and absorbing its dozens of principles, you may wonder: What is Joan's strongest personal guiding principle? It is: "Make it happen."

For that reason, when I wrap up a speech or training session, I always ask my audience to tell me what it is that we've discussed that they can really use; that way I can find out if I've been an effective lecturer and coach.

Hearing from readers will therefore help me know if *Communication by Design* has achieved its mission. I would welcome hearing how you personally relate to the principles throughout this book. Has anything in particular made a difference for you? How have *you* applied these specific principles? Or modified them for your own circumstances? What might you like to see in a future book?

I am already collecting principles and anecdotes for further use; I would be pleased to know and consider yours. After all, I am still learning, along with everyone else.

My e-mail is jcapelin@capelin.com; don't hesitate to contact me.

I wish you the very best.

Joan Capelin, FSMPS, Hon. AIA, Fellow PRSA
New York City
April 2004

PRINCIPLE 1

Define *success*

How do you know what a particular client wants? Since 1996, the American Society of Interior Designers (ASID) has been tackling this prickly question. The society's strategic-mapping research was conceived to help designers to communicate—and thus work better—with their clients. For instance, when clients say, "You really know what I need," ASID wondered, *do* you?

ASID's research has revealed critical language gaps. "Cost control" to designers meant staying within the preset budget. But to their clients, it meant optimizing and justifying the budget, whatever that ultimately amounts to. The designers wanted to save their clients money, while the clients wanted to know the *real* costs of the project and to make strategic decisions about what they would spend, given those real costs.

Clients and designers are not at cross-purposes; they each want the other to succeed, and most want a genuinely creative, collaborative effort. Clients may not be smart about design and construction, but usually they know what their own business needs are.

If everything you are hired to do should advance your clients' goals, how do you learn what the goals are and how the clients expect (you) to achieve them?

Just ask them.

Try out a few questions:

What will it take to say that the job is a success?

What is important to you? The way things look? A set dead-line? The money involved?

What does your organization want to achieve here? What constituencies also have to be satisfied?

What would you like to add to this briefing?

What feedback can you give us?

While developing a new business relationship, you probably have asked why the prospective client wanted a particular building or place, what long-range benefits he anticipated, and why he would spend his money this way. It should be natural to continue in this querying mode after the job is won.

Questioning can start early. Immediately upon job *acceptance*, you can ask for a debriefing to learn why you were hired for the project. You may be surprised. All too often, debriefing occurs when a job is lost; even if you ask why the other firm won, it's rare that you get the entire answer. But for you to be considered effective in the client's eyes, it is essential to know the reasons why you won the opportunity and why another firm didn't.

Barton Malow, the national construction company, has a remarkable Customer Satisfaction Program and report card. At the start of every job, the Barton Malow project manager conducts an interview with the client and completes a Client Expectation Report. Each month or quarter, whichever the client prefers, the client and Barton Malow meet again so the client can rate his level of satisfaction according to the expectations that were defined and communicated at the beginning of the project.

Barton Malow doesn't stop there. The company prepares an executive summary that repeats back to the client what the company has been told—to be sure that everyone agrees with at the end of the job; the company wants to know before the job—or the damage—is done.

Firms often don't know there is a problem until a former client refuses to give a good reference. To keep the information flowing, one firm sends reply cards with its invoices, to be returned to the company president. The reply card asks, "How are we doing?" One firm of engineers in the Northwest uses an Internet-based feedback system it has perfected.

Questioning isn't limited to the firm's owners. Others all along the chain can easily be involved. The lead financial person, for instance, can ask the client counterpart if invoices are clear and complete, and what could be done to speed the bill review process. A project manager's unspoken job is to identify issues and conflicts regarding the project, especially in the field. Asking his counterpart in the client company about these issues, as well as inquiring about the client's level of satisfaction, will certainly trap the problems as they occur.

Marketers are well suited for ongoing client relations because they are trained to be active listeners. They constantly read about developments in the client's world. By asking all the right questions, they may have identified, researched, and reeled in the job. And they should be adept at debriefing. In fact, the job description for a marketer should flag these desirable skills.

Marketing managers who have maintained contact with the client are in an excellent, neutral position to monitor the project's success. They might ask:

What is your understanding of our commitments? How well are we delivering on them?

Do you feel that you are getting value for the money?

How do our fees compare with those of other consultants?

What is your own risk on this project?

If you had it to do over again, how would you have wanted this job done?

Would you give us a positive reference?

If our firm were *your* business, what would you do differently?

What else can we help you with now?

But here's the rub: When you get your answers, you must be prepared to deliver on the feedback. It is important for both your clients and your staff to see that you are responsive and committed to your principles.

One firm that gathers this information has a Client Review Committee that meets monthly to assess client relationships, find ways to prevent dissatisfaction, and—let's not forget this—identify new service opportunities.

Corollary: Ask your clients how *they* are doing, individually and as an organization. Their answers may offer new opportunities or reveal a new set of expectations of you. Good to know, either way.

Play by your client's rules

The best possible validation comes from your client's endorsement—but not all clients want to give your work and presence visibility, let alone credit.

In fact, some clients don't want the project mentioned until the doors are ready to open or at least until demolition begins. They reason that there are too many opposing interests "out there," some of them well-trained and well-organized groups.

In one case, our client's client, a major utility, summoned us to its offices to review its requirements in person. At the same time that its new headquarters was going into the ground, it had announced a rate increase, something never well received. The utility wanted to be sure that the design and building team didn't tell the public about the project, least of all its size and cost. Even though the new structure was one million square feet and located next to a major highway overpass with a clear view of the site, these folks still wanted to be sure that we did not call attention to the job.

In another instance, a high-visibility designer joyfully showed a restaurant design to a prominent architecture editor, who, relishing the scoop, published the sketches immediately. But the owner believed that the architect, by exposing the fact of that restaurant, which was to be a major new business for a food-processing company, had seriously breached the company's confidential marketing plan. Imagine the lawsuit that ensued.

The first clue about a client's attitude is in the contract. See if the contract gives you permission to use the project to bring attention to your firm or his. Not there? Then introduce the topic during the negotiations and get the ground rules clarified—preferably in writing, if not in the contract itself. If you don't take this step, even with the best of clients, misunderstandings can lead to fireworks later.

Is there language about clearance, for instance? Is it clear that the client will credit you each time the building is used for its own promotions? Will you be able to photograph the work upon completion? What if your access to the property is restricted after the job is completed?

This may not be contractual, but nonetheless it pays to ask about the clearance procedure for any written piece used for your own marketing and public relations. Who should be quoted in the press release: the president? key user? head of facilities? project manager?

What is your client's personality: loose or controlling? One architecture office innocently proposed a conference program that included two highly placed "users" from its institutional client on the panel. When the director of facilities learned about the proposal, he demanded that the architects withdraw it.

What had our hapless architects done wrong? They hadn't asked the director of facilities first. Was this in their contract? Were there any instructions up to that point, already a year into the project? Not even mentioned. Then what crime was committed? The architects had considered the *user* to be their client. "Wrong!" the director of facilities reminded them: *He* was the client.

What concerned me most about this last anecdote is that the architects apologized, when only regrets were called for. If something were to go truly wrong in the future, how could they respond? Their mistake was inadvertent; the client's reaction was disproportionate, though in keeping with his volatile personality. "We regret what happened. We would like to meet with you to define how you would like your architecture consultants to act in the future," would have recalibrated the relationship and enabled them to continue the project compliantly, not submissively.

Bottom line: It's wise to consider whose money, reputation, and/or job is on the line. Even though designing projects or construction may be your reason for being in business, your work is a means to your client's ends. If you want to talk about the project during and after the work is done, get this spelled out—and *still* be careful as you progress.

PRINCIPLE 3

It's not the problem itself but how you handle the problem that will be remembered

Dealing with bad news is really quite straightforward. There are four classic Rs: Regret. Rectification. Restitution. Reform. True reform. Don't apologize for something and then do it again. Everyone makes mistakes; the trick is not getting known for it.

Delivering bad news to a client is an art that every principal must master. No matter the magnitude of the problem, in the long run it's not the problem itself but how you handle it that will be remembered.

You must inform three essential constituencies immediately: the leadership involved, the client, and your staff. The first step is to move quickly to alert your company's leadership and agree on the extent of the trouble, as well as what's at stake for the firm, how prepared you are to fix the problem, and what your plan is to do so.

Then inform the client: the facts, how the damage has been or could be controlled, and how you are dealing with it. Everyone in your client's organization whom you surprise with bad news has someone else *he* must surprise. Enable everyone to say, and believe, "The situation is under control."

Next, tell your staff. And stand by them. At this point, it does no good to blame anyone, nor, frankly, to assume that the problem is of your firm's making.

Your client's perception of what is at risk may differ from yours; it's best to get this clarified. Here's an example at the extreme end of what constitutes a problem. I recall one roof collapse—no one was there when it happened, fortunately—where the distressed client barred the entire design team from the site and left himself to deal with the cleanup, alone. The engineers who knew how to rectify the situation were justifiably doubly upset: by the event and by having their offer of assistance shunned.

For the editor at *Engineering News-Record*, the story of the lockout was the nugget she wanted; the collapse was more ordinary for her. By explaining the problem in detail to the *ENR* editor—including the offer and the rebuff—we were able to get the design team's story minimal and balanced coverage.

Obviously, problems come in all sizes. Bob Hillier of The Hillier Group is very straightforward on the issue of bad news. He counsels that you can save client relationships by the simple acknowledgment that you did not do something correctly and that you are prepared to fix it. No job is perfect, he admits, yet he has seen architects go into a "defensive, hard-to-pin-down mode that angers all clients."

"In at least a dozen cases over the years," Bob explains, "our assertive, 'let's-solve-this-problem-now' approach has resulted in further work from the same client and references where the client has told others about our 'excellent responsiveness.'"

Avoiding a problem is inappropriate and even unethical. Project managers must acknowledge bad news, explain their role in it, and immediately bring the situation to the attention of the responsible principal. What if an employee doesn't tell you about a problem, or a group covers up a situation? Speak to each employee separately. Warn him once, loud and clear. Get the facts of this warning in writing, in his employee file, and on his desk. If another cover-up occurs, he clearly does not want to live up to the standards of his profession. He should be shown the door.

PRINCIPLE 4

If you don't ask, you don't get

One of the most valuable lessons I learned about marketing happened at the Copacabana Club on East 60th Street in New York City. In the 1990s, the club had reopened and was renting its space to business groups at lunchtime. Naturally, the New York component of the Society for Marketing Professional Services began to hold its regular monthly meetings there.

One month, the speaker was one of those inspirational types who usually make me antsy, but I was a good trooper. I wasn't alone: He attracted a total of eleven tables with ten seats each.

Once on stage, our speaker asked casually if each of us had a dollar bill, and if so, would we hold it up? Some had no singles, only fives, tens or twenties. "That's okay," he reassured us.

He instructed us to put our bills in the center of the table, and he asked one of the members to go around the room to collect each pile. When he came to our table, ten hands went down to protect the cache; no way was he getting *our* money. "That's okay," the speaker repeated, in the same calm voice.

He then asked our colleague to bring him the wad of bills. A hundred-plus singles make a substantial fistful of money. He held it up high. And then he said something remarkably obvious: "If you don't ask, you don't get."

He, of course, returned the money after lunch. I have always thought he should have kept the money: It would have been a cheap price for learning a very important principle.

How many businesses suffer because their principals haven't asked for something? Perhaps a higher fee that would give the firm some breathing room? A change in the consulting team that would avoid a conflict or raise the quality of the work? Better terms on reproduction services for marketing materials? An evergreen contract?

In 1997 one of our clients, Taliesin Architects, designed a "Dream House" for the May issue of *LIFE* magazine. This comfortable home—rather, six versions of a home that would be site-specific in the best traditions of "organic architecture"— was the design of the great Frank Lloyd Wright apprentice John Rattenbury.

R. Nicholas "Ryc" Loope, then at the helm of Taliesin Architects, had previously invited me to work with him on a marketing and public relations strategy for the firm, including this wonderful project. Ryc had a Dream House built in secrecy in the Rockies, so there was something real to photograph. An outstanding editorial staff that really understood the design intent completed the article, and both the artwork and the shoot were excellent. The issue of *LIFE* was all but wrapped up, and Taliesin Architects was to have the cover.

But then *LIFE* decided to lead with a story about children who suffered from asthma and allergies. I would argue that a gorgeous house, priced so it was available to most people, would be a more appealing cover. Obviously, the magazine disagreed, and so we lost the cover.

By then, we knew the *LIFE* people fairly well. Our materials to promote both the May issue and sales of the house plans didn't depend on our providing the cover, but having it would have helped the campaign immeasurably. With nothing to lose,

I asked the *LIFE* people if they would give us the right to use the cover that didn't happen—possibly my wildest request ever. Yes, the folks in the art department made 100 copies for us. Our very own use of the famed *LIFE* logo!

One personal anecdote further demonstrates this principle: Not long ago, my family was in Bogotá for a wedding. Everything was enchanting—including a foot-tall, pre-Colombian amphora that graced the console in the vestibule of our hotel floor. As we were waiting for the elevator to leave for home, I commented that I would really miss the piece, which had the delicious shape of a chubby, small man. Then I sighed and went to check out.

My daughter, Lauren, who has often heard the Copacabana anecdote, taunted me: "Mother, if you don't ask, you don't get." Won't work, I crisply told her; no hotel sells its artwork.

Still, my credibility was at stake, so I asked. The front desk parried, but one of our family members vigorously supported my request in rapid-fire Spanish. After a few minutes of this (and, let it be said, a legitimate payment), the head housekeeper graciously had the statuette boxed for the trip to the States. Today *"Señor Si No Preguntas, No Recibes"* sits at my desk, a captivating reminder of a lovely trip and also the usefulness of speaking up.

PRINCIPLE 5

FUBB

Let me pass on the excellent advice of Bill Fife, most recently the aviation practice leader and corporate vice president at DMJM + Harris. Years ago, when Bill was still planning airports for the Port Authority of New York and New Jersey, he taught me to FUBB—Follow-Up Beyond Belief!

Every day, I use this powerful acronym. Even in an industry where "God is in the details" and where an omission from a working drawing affects life and safety, FUBBing does not come naturally.

For instance:

Does your marketing manager FUBB to be sure that the proposal or awards submission has arrived on the desk of the person for whom it is intended, and that it is complete? To learn what will be the next steps required, and when?

Does your accounting department FUBB ten days after the bill goes out, to be sure it has been received and reviewed? To inquire if there are issues that could delay its payment?

Does your chief financial person call the new client ten days after the new contract is signed, to introduce herself (or celebrate the reconnection) and learn whether the client's accounting department knows there is a contract in play? And to learn whether your proposed billing process conforms to theirs?

Does your staff write down the name of every person they have either met on a job or who might give you a job; and does your staff automatically provide the names to the keeper of your master mailing list, so the firm can FUBB with the client or prospect?

Do your project managers or administrators FUBB the day after the minutes are delivered, to ensure that all the people named have received their copy and agree on what is expected within the designated time frame?

When you've been interviewed for an article, do you FUBB to be sure that the editor has everything he needs and was clear on what you said? That the promised photo or graphic has reached his desk? And when the article appears and is reasonably close to what was said in the interview, do you FUBB with a thank-you note?

Do you contact and thank the people who refer business to you—and FUBB as the referral advances toward a new client relationship?

One engineering firm's COO would call and FUBB his firm's clients punctually every day: Is there anything you need from us? Is everything going on schedule? Are our people performing? The person who told me this anecdote was the recipient of these daily FUBBs. He even would make up an answer, just to end the call. However, he divulged, having an interested and vigilant consultant gave him enormous confidence in the project and the design team.

FUBBing doesn't stop when the project ends. One Washington, D.C.-based group of interior architects does formal FUBBing, although they call it a post-occupancy survey. At no cost to the client, near the first anniversary of the move-in (and before the guarantees expire), they go back and officially examine the results of their work, to assess its durability, consider the effectiveness of the design, and stop any problems

before they become destructive both to the job and the relationship.

"We observe how finishes are wearing, whether more atten-
tive maintenance programs are needed, and coincidentally,
whether the client has any new issues we can help him to
address," explains Marilyn Burroughs, president of Blue Chair
Design (a division of WDG). "They love to see that we continued to take a proprietary interest in them and their space,
even after the contract is complete." Of course, at the same
time, Marilyn learns about changes in the client's organization
and thus new opportunities she could explore and develop.

Weld Coxe coined the phrase "Old Business Development,"
for strategic ways to FUBB by keeping a former client in range
and in the family. Clients are like your investment portfolio—
they offer a source of more work, references, physical proof of
your good efforts, and awards, among other benefits. Here are
some ways you can FUBB:

Consider an exit interview: Ask what the client would do differently next time? What should our firm be doing differently?
Then implement the most feasible of these suggestions—and
report back to the client about your progress.

Orchestrate ways to stay in touch with past clients. Clients
come at all levels: chairman, president, CEO, CFO, project
manager. Assign their counterpart in your organization to track
them.

One housekeeping note: Many firms rely on direct mail to
stay in touch with past clients—which is good, but it does not
yield feedback or news. There is nothing like one-on-one, personal contact when people have been so important to you.

PRINCIPLE 6

Treat your clients the way you would treat friends

Sixpence in Her Shoe is a book of essays by the mid-twentieth-century poet Phyllis McGinley. I read the *Sixpence* chapter titled "Manners Make Morals" to our young daughter and to any other child who would listen. The chapter's entire message, charmingly told, is in its title.

Neither McGinley's essay nor this principle is about prissy manners. Her point was that being courteous to others is a sign of respect. My old-fashioned contribution is to feature some fundamental, memorable actions that people, especially businesspeople under pressure, are often too preoccupied to consider.

Take, for instance, this story about Carla Thompson, former marketing director at Hart Crowser, a Seattle-based firm of consulting engineers. Carla reasoned that people deal best with people they like and trust, so she instituted a note-writing campaign. Her goal was to enhance relationships with her firm's clients, which might make them more loyal.

Carla encouraged the firm's different divisions to write notes to their clients. The engineers would send her a photocopy. She also provided personalized corporate stationery for them so they could pen: "*Congratulations!*" "*Thank you for the job.*" "*Great to see you well again.*" "*Exciting news about Little League!*"

And here's one never-seen-before message, six months into a job: "*We really like working with you; you're a great project manager.*"

Carla found that everyone got into the spirit and all were prolific writers. She threw an officewide party to thank and encourage them. As it turned out, their clients loved getting the mail; some even posted it. Her conclusion? "The campaign gave 'civil engineers' new meaning."

Dennis Paoletti is another considerate letter writer. An acoustics and A/V consultant trained as an architect, he does something exceptional that, on reflection, seems so obvious: He sends an introductory letter as the project begins, thanking the client for the assignment.

Years back, Long Island architect John Sorrenti shared his perspective on client relationships: "Client marketing is most successful when you look at it as acquiring new friends. How you react to your friends is how you should react to your clients." Although we have all been warned of the perils of mixing friendships or family with business, there is no interdiction about *finding* friendship within a business context. Working people with busy lives will admit that many of their friendships are with the clients, consultants, and vendors they see day-in, day-out through their work.

I began to observe how some of the best principals and marketers "befriended" their clients. They would start by learning about the client's life beyond the project. They would make a mental list of the client's family members and track their milestones—graduation, new job titles, surgery, whatever—as they would for their own personal friends. From this, solid relationships grew.

Joel Merker, for one instance, heads a small New York firm that specializes in interior architecture. I observed that Joel had raised the bar on client relationships: His clients all became friends, not just repeat clients. However, this became a marketing challenge: How can you do a standard brochure or newsletter to stay in touch, when you have such close relationships? How do you remind friends that they are also a source of business? Instead, we worked with Joel on a letter to update his growing community on what was happening in the Merker office.

At a time when work was generally slowing, Joel sent out a letter whose theme was, "Thanks to you, we're busy—and we're doing this excellent work." We slipped in some project pictures, and Joel penned notes in the margin to personalize the letters. Even though it was fairly obvious that this was a form letter with a commercial purpose, people actually wrote back, and the work continued to flow.

One sparkling architect, Maria Wilpon, a principal at Helpern Architects, thoroughly enjoys meeting people—who are, to the rest of us, prospective clients. Curious about other people, positive, and always enthusiastic, she brings them into her warm, and by definition large, circle of friends. Maria has made me believe that, for some people, business can quite naturally lead to delightful friendships.

Still, the first time she told me that she had shown pictures of her family to a client, I was taken aback. But the client proudly responded by showing *his* family's pictures, knowing that Maria would be delighted. That taught me a big and welcome lesson—in fact, permitted me to change the way I approach people.

Returning to the leitmotif of letter campaigns, which supports the theme of "celebrate client relationships," here are a few tips that will mark you as a thoughtful person:

Keep by your pencil cup a stack of postcards, perhaps with views of your office's work or of other well-designed buildings—silos to skyscrapers—that you find on commercial cards. Send a brief message to someone every day. Lower postage, great goodwill.

Congratulate the president of an organization or its conference chair when an event goes well—even if you don't know that person, and especially if you were one of the speakers. If you've run a program or meeting and only gotten a form letter to acknowledge the hours of hard work, you know what I mean.

Write and tell the individual members of a design jury how much the award you received matters to your staff and client. It's not hard to get those addresses. If you've ever served on a jury, you know what a challenging labor of love that is. Needless to say, it's the jury's time and thoughtfulness you are acknowledging, not your selection by the jury for the award.

Perform random acts of kindness. If what goes 'round *does* come 'round, this is an especially rewarding point to remember.

PRINCIPLE 7

Treat your associated firms the way you would treat friends

Why is it so hard for design professionals to share credit for work done with another firm? It should be easy—not just professional and ethical—to show mutual respect for the talent and effort of colleagues.

I have always insisted that, when the work involves more than one firm, credit must be given to all whenever and wherever it is due. Appropriate credit needs to appear in the project press release, project fact sheet, brochure page, Web site section, award submission, and any oral presentation. Always indicate who is involved and in what way.

I encourage firms that affiliate on projects to put in writing in their initiating agreement how they expect the credits to read and who will control the publicity for the project—and also to make sure that all members of the project team and their respective marketing people know the terms. Ditto for the contract with the project owner.

While I could provide dozens of examples of supportive relationships between firms—some offices thrive on this model— nonetheless, these courtesies sometimes are left behind. "Why should *we* do it," I'm challenged, "when the other firm hasn't given us credit?" But that's not hard to remedy: Ask those in the other firm to play nicely. Usually, they do—at least when they are caught in the act.

Attribution issues span project types and firm sizes. I've seen big firms, and even some of the most noted ones, consciously excise associated firms or critical consultants from submissions to magazines or for awards. Editors or juries on tight schedules can't always check the facts. But eventually, these shenanigans surface; word gets around.

ArchNewsNow.com's founder and editor, Kristen Richards, tells the story of a small firm that put out a news release about a wonderful project. She was amazed that such a large-scale job, excellently conceived and delivered, could have been the result of that small firm's work. Scrolling down to the very last sentence, she found a brief mention about the architects whose project it really was. As it turns out, the small firm was a *bona fide* consultant for its small portion of the project, but the release had misrepresented it as prime. Kristen's knowledge of the industry enabled her to catch the misrepresentation; unfortunately, other editors might not be so vigilant or curious.

"Good fences make good neighbors," wrote Robert Frost. If nothing is agreed on and documented, then even an innocent misstep could damage the team; you must speak up about the problem before it gets out of hand.

In this next example, you'll see how the failure to define a project's publicity in writing led to a mountain of misunderstanding. A magazine article celebrated a job well done: the sensitive integration of a retail establishment into a salvaged, nearly derelict historic building. The story deservedly praised the interior architect. But it relegated the core-and-shell architect to eight-point type with the single credit of "exterior architect." Yet the exterior architect had actually made the project possible by identifying the opportunity, bringing in the developer, ensuring the city's agreement, stabilizing and restoring the façade, and collaborating on the interiors.

How did this omission happen? The featured designer, who was the interior architect, told the editor to speak to the "owner" about how the project began and ended; in the designer's mind, the "owner" was the owner of the retail establishment, the designer's client. But the *real* owner was the developer, the client of the unheralded exterior architect—and so an exemplary story of design entrepreneurship went untold. The editor did not ask about the ultimate client or where the story had begun. In short, faced with the probability that the project merited major coverage, neither the exterior nor the interior architecture firms moved to discuss and agree in writing about *project* publicity that would have benefited both offices.

To avoid having the dispute between two affiliated offices for project credits spill over onto the project owner's or editor's desk, I have at times—when I know both firms—personally intervened. Last time I did so, a little too late in the situation, my client was so pugnacious in the meeting, I was concerned that he would physically deck his counterpart. It became clear where the problem had really started.

In another instance—this one with a lucky ending—an unexpected dispute about project credit didn't surface for a dozen years. The Web site of a regional campus museum, whose expansion had presaged a spurt in reputation as well as in attendance, stated that the building had been designed by a name architect, since deceased.

Actually, the commission had been won by a firm that had begun with this contract. This firm had, in time-honored tradition, affiliated with the deceased star architect—but ultimately the design, production work, and "architect of record" status belonged to the new firm. Belatedly, the architects found that the legendary name alone survived in the museum's memory.

Speaking finally to the museum's new director, whom the architecture firm had never contacted, the architects calmly explained the situation. We helped them structure their request in such a way that not only did they get things straightened out, but they were also encouraged to update their qualifications with the university and thus resume the disrupted relationship.

Yet another situation did not end as well. Two firms affiliated to design a university's new business school facility. Signature work, campus reorientation, new definition of academic building—all the good stuff made for developing the firms' expertise and reputation, and, let it be said, further marketing. Except that one of the two firms didn't want to continue developing business jointly. When both firms pursued another business school opportunity, one of them took sole credit for the project (an unethical and potentially damaging decision). Rather than figuring out who did what, the university decided not to consider either firm.

One of the lost talents of our times, not just in this industry, is the ability to apologize. Who hasn't been cut off by the switchboard, only to call back and get attitude? Or learned late that a consultant's drawings wouldn't be delivered on time—but then been stonewalled by the behind-schedule team member? I recall this caustic, pertinent quote from François de La Rochefoucauld, the seventeenth-century French author: "Almost all our faults are more pardonable than the methods we employ to hide them."

PRINCIPLE 8

Lose well

The era of courtesy is receding rapidly. We have become a surly nation of litigious, bat-flinging, teacher-threatening, bad-mouthing, sore losers.

Certainly, this behavior makes banner headlines and powerful theatrical scripts. But you can't win 'em all, and winning is—surprisingly—not the only way to become memorable. Sometimes you can lose well.

Occasionally, someone will hand me a letter received from a worthy competitor: "I just learned that our office did not succeed in getting the job we were both going after. However, I was *delighted* to hear that your office got the commission. The client is in good hands. Congratulations!" Could there be any kinder words from another professional?

If you've lost, it's entirely possible that the other team may have really done its homework, figured out the politics, come in with an attractive funding source—or just been better suited.

Or, to look at the positive side, perhaps the review committee only wanted to get a sense of who you were so you could be considered for another project. That's why I always counsel people who are going into competitive presentations to relax: you never know what job you're really up for, so you might as well enjoy the encounter.

This is a call to your inner Dan O'Brien. O'Brien is the 1996 Olympic decathlon athlete with a strong sense of himself and an equally strong sense of humor who lost very publicly at the pole vault and almost every other event—but captured everyone's affection for the way he subsequently conducted himself.

Ted Hammer, senior managing partner of HLW International, doesn't like to lose an opportunity, but he manages even that part of the business development process beneficially. As one story goes, a major high-tech company was looking for an architect, considered HLW, and then went with another firm. Ted sent his contact a note wishing him the best, telling him that, although HLW was keenly disappointed, Ted respected the firm that was chosen.

He didn't stop there. Ted, who has an eye for grown-up toys, sent this man a soft sculpture of a sad face: "That's what we feel like," read the card. For two years, it was on display in that executive's office—at which point HLW was offered the assignment to be master planners and architects for the company's entire region.

Mind your netiquette

E-mail is no longer a casual, innocent tool. Who hasn't received or heard a story about an unintended e-mail message that had serious consequences? It is perilously easy to hit the "Send" key and, in a stroke, cancel a business relationship. "Reply to All," in particular, is the devil's own work.

Appreciated for its speed, convenience, and informality, e-mail has taken over our offices. It rapidly connects an organization to its clients, vendors, and friends. But it can just as rapidly broadcast privileged information about your business. Think what a disaffected employee can do with a keystroke. (Think, too, how quickly that person's corporate e-mail account should be closed, if he is about to be released to industry.)

In court cases, e-mails are now considered as valid as interoffice memos. The American Management Association (AMA) reported in 2003 that 14 percent of companies surveyed had been "ordered by a court or regulatory body to produce employee e-mail." E-mails can easily escalate into hand-to-hand combat, providing great fodder for formal or informal chat rooms, chopping up a company's hard-won reputation. Because of this, an e-mail policy is a very good idea for any business. In fact, get it into the office manual, post it, and enforce it in training sessions.

My special concern is that each correspondent seems entirely independent and responsible for the content, accuracy, intelligence, tone, and storage of his electronic correspondence.

There is no extra pair of eyes to proofread the text or to caution the sender. Many people don't even know that you can print a draft version of outgoing e-mail. General correspondence produced on paper—letters, memos, minutes, and the like—is at least subject to office graphics, scrutiny, and policies regarding what needs to be copied for the office files. But e-mail eludes these procedures.

Facing facts, this new generation of professionals—despite its fine education—has not gone out of its way to master spelling and grammar. Some people in the notoriously nonverbal design and construction industry are even proud of that distinction. Electronic correspondence seems to further liberate them from the need to consult a grammar stylebook or dictionary, enabling them to respond curtly, not to mention innocent of capital letters.

Understandably, clients favor e-mail because it's faster, can be accessed at all hours, saves postage, and avoids unproductive telephone-tagging. As we advance into the BlackBerry Era, when information will also be transmitted remotely, documenting decisions and permissions conveyed electronically will become ever more difficult to achieve.

Not all clients and prospects want to receive marketing materials via the Internet. One marketing department with which we worked balked when we encouraged it to set up an e-mail list, because the members of marketing group, themselves, disliked receiving unsolicited e-mail—even something useful. Since an online publication was part of the agreed-upon marketing strategy for the office, we needed to get past this stumbling block.

We convinced them to send a letter to all the people on their mailing list via real mail with a stamped return postcard enclosed, asking recipients to verify their land address and to grant permission to use the Internet for reasons other than project correspondence. Many provided this contact information, though not all. Glad we asked.

One problem with e-mail is attachments. Sometimes they are so large that they may take ages to download—high-resolution visuals, for instance, can tie up even high-speed lines for interminable periods. This is truly onerous for people who pay by the hour for their Internet service. A city agency director once instructed us to e-mail photographs to her resident graphic designer before a presentation. Yet the art department didn't have the capacity (or software) to receive them. Better to ask the actual recipient first.

Not all editors like to receive information electronically, either. For them, we make sure that the subject line explains the nature of the message. We also check to see whether they can receive photos and text in the format we have available, and whether they will open attachments. (For security reasons, some publications have stopped opening attachments.)

Mass mailings are so much easier by e-mail, but who wants to receive one with three pages of addresses for a two-line message? "Blind carbon copy" is the correct mode. In fact, the next time you do a mass mailing, do a dry run to yourself and a few colleagues in-house to be sure you have the hang of it. People value their privacy; do all you can to protect it.

If you are asking for a response to your mass mailing, provide the link in the body of the message. This avoids having the recipient respond to the entire group. People have been known to remove themselves from association Listservs out of frustration, after they have been copied with every single contact—oh, how they mushroom! This is certainly not the intended result.

Finally, e-mail may be the worst time thief out there, far beyond the klatch around the proverbial cooler. Ninety percent of the AMA survey respondents admitted that they send and receive personal e-mails at work. AMA's measured comment was that this certainly "compounds the problem."

PRINCIPLE 10

Get the right picture

Why don't architecture photo shoots achieve what they are supposed to? If a picture is worth a thousand words, and if a good architecture photographer charges well over a thousand dollars a day, the math alone reveals how important it is to maximize the shoot.

One reason a photo shoot fails is that the person who designed the project doesn't see it the way it actually turned out, but rather the way he *wanted* it to turn out. Some photographers can interpret a space, some will record it faithfully, but none can show what isn't there. Captions—another art—can't fudge it, either. Thus, the first step is to define what you want the shoot to achieve. The second is to be realistic about what you have to work with.

Another reason for disappointment is that some excellent places and spaces simply don't translate well photographically—and that includes Gold Medal–quality work. What's more, having people in the photo is essential for some places to come alive photographically; this contradicts the tradition of many design publications and awards juries, which historically have selected unpopulated photos.

It is critical to list all of the intended uses of the shoot. Imagine every possible way you might explain the place and your work, as though you, yourself, were walking your prospective client or an editor through it. Jot down every anecdote you already tell about it. What views support this dialogue?

Other useful questions to ask yourself before turning the shoot over to the photographer:

How is this project—and, therefore, group of photos—going to help me get more work?

What messages do I want the photos to convey?: How much more quickly people heal in, say, a patient-centered health-care space? How office production has soared? How ingeniously a new technology has been integrated? Or, how effective I am with small, signature spaces (or large-footprint buildings)?

Do I have all the necessary views for new-business presentations, lectures, awards submissions, display panels, articles, and proposals?

For how much of this do I have the budget? Could the photographer take candid slides or use a digital camera for secondary views—click! click!—reserving the bulk of the time contracted for the most significant views?

How well will the photographer I've chosen be able to mirror my interests?

Photography for publication must work very hard. Editors rarely travel anymore to see the projects they write about, so to replace the walk-through, the photos must be not only outstanding but also informative. To demonstrate context, features, and effect, it is good to script the shoot and require—despite the cost—more than the glory shots.

This story about getting a project into print recounts how I learned what "intended use" really means to a publication. Within a project portfolio that I had taken to the art director of a hospitality design publication was a glorious, inviting view of a hotel's grounds, shot from the doorway leading to a well-

styled veranda with an elegant colonnade. I told the art director how I envisioned the magazine's logo positioned across the
tall columns, just below their ornate capitals. I imagined cover
copy legibly placed over the open-sky vista and the adjacent
landscape. (I also imagined the pleasure of telling our client
that this exquisite photograph would be on the cover.)

The art director disabused me of my enthusiasm for the photograph. "Pick what will make the target reader grab the magazine from the rack," he instructed. "What's *that*? is the desired
impulse." The cover photo he selected was of the hotel's heavi-
ly decorated, double-height dining room. You couldn't easily
read the cover copy because there was so much ornament—but
without question, it was arresting.

Lighting designers need to be especially alert when their
work is photographed, particularly if they want to use the photographs in their own professional portfolios. The lighting
effect in an interior space may not readily translate onto film,
without a photographer's "correction." What the eye sees in a
live space, and what the camera records on film, may differ
without this intervention.

When an interior space is photographed, it is usually the
architect who contracts with the photographer—for the architect's benefit—to show off the best qualities of the architect's
work. The photographer will, therefore, correct the light for the
architect's purposes. In the process, the lighting designer's work
may be sacrificed or at least not be obvious in the photographs.

Some photographers are better with natural light than others, and some photographers are superb at creating—or re-cre-
ating—special lighting effects. Either way, a lighting designer
who is not financially involved in the shoot will probably not

have the opportunity to make his particular wishes known. It is to the lighting designer's advantage to find his own photographer, one who will understand these issues and who can accurately replicate the lighting designer's art on film. This way, the lighting designer can ensure the best possible photographs for himself and his portfolio.

Landscape photography can also fail. I surprised one landscape photographer by instructing her to show the key *buildings* in the work of a particular landscape architect—not the landscapes devoid of structures. Our client needed the shoot to be compelling to architects who could hire his firm as a subconsultant. Further, I wanted the photographer to demonstrate more than how the hard and soft landscapes complemented the buildings; I wanted her to enable us to feel the temperature of the place and hear the natural sounds of that setting. What an extraordinary shoot she gave us!

Instead of using a single approach for a shoot, consider photographing the project in different ways. For one architecture shoot of a private bank set in a McKim Mead & White town house, the design firm had elected to do the banking floor in the most modern style. But the offices, themselves, closely resembled the original century-old décor, part of the bank's strategy to attract well-heeled clients. Because the architects intended to use the photos to market their historic preservation services as well as their high-tech banking design, we orchestrated two shoots, with two different set-ups, with the same photographer: one shoot was done with lighting that befitted the landmark quality of the building, and the other shoot represented the entire building as a new bank in an uncommon setting.

Have I emphasized "context" strongly enough? You must include additional views that show the context of the project. First, many awards and honors programs demand those views, and second, just for the richness of your exposition, you need a record of the surroundings. It's imperative to show where the project is located, even for an interiors project. Nothing is designed and built in a vacuum.

Remember these tips:

The principal involved must be on-site at least at the start of the shoot to revisit with the photographer the previously provided shoot script and views list, and to enlist the help of the maintenance people. Your interest and involvement spur on the photographer, who has a long haul ahead.

While you're on the site, you might take the opportunity to get a staged picture of yourself there. Ask the photographer to accommodate you. People in the design world often try to look artistic or blasé in indoor shots, but then end up looking distant and bored. All, however, look vibrant when captured on film around construction they have caused to happen.

Select one great photograph of the finished work and present it, matted and framed, to the owner and/or key client representative for his office wall—with your company's name and perhaps your signature penned on the matting, of course. If the client is an institution, it might happily buy that same view from you to give to its major donor, or may certainly use the shoot in its development materials.

PRINCIPLE 11

The journey is as important as the arrival

It's nice to get clients, and sometimes nice to leave them. Since you don't always control when that happens, you might as well enjoy the time you spend together. Here are some ideas:

1. Celebrate achievements.

The tendency in this industry is to come down hard on errors, but not to recognize how much has been accomplished, how far you've come. Some people claim this intense attitude starts with the crits and juries review process in design school. Time to leave that behind.

It ought to be a genuine pleasure to commemorate the occasion when a significant phase in a project is complete—for instance, when the client signs off on the design or the drawings go out to bid. Observe the moment, with the client.

But then also celebrate with your team. As you organize the job, tap the milestones into your Palm Pilot; the rest should be simple.

One Arizona architect told me his philosophy: "Clients tend to remember their first and last experiences, and forget much of the middle, so you should make sure that the first and last encounters are fantastic. However, each service encounter you have with your client is—for the time being, anyway—the last. Make it positive and memorable."

2. Orchestrate the experience.

In a case study about integrated marketing communications, I read how Saturn created good feelings about the company and its cars. Early on, Saturn shaped its marketing around a simple strategy for making the customer feel comfortable and well served. Before the first car came off the assembly line, Saturn's management had a list of forty defining moments in the customer relationship cycle—starting when the customer first saw the ad for the car, came to the showroom, drove away with the new car, returned for servicing, and, ultimately, traded in the car for a newer one. And then Saturn's managers considered how to manage each of these moments, making sure that they were true to the mission of the company.

This drill brought together every person in the company: the factory workers, the financial people, the sales and service staff, and the technicians. That's how Saturn created customer loyalty.

What if your office were to consider the hundreds of times that your staff comes into contact with your clients and potential clients: on the phone, at the door, in the field or in your office, at meetings, at business and social functions, as well as in the mail, through the Internet, and when they receive your invoice. Are those moments of contact "positive and memorable"?

Forty years ago, Mary Kay Ash created a remarkable cosmetics business that gave many women a chance to become self-supporting, not just to own a pink Cadillac. This Mary Kay quote reveals her approach: "Everyone has an invisible sign hanging from her neck saying, 'Make me feel important.'"

3. Make a strong first impression.

A 250-person multidiscipline firm was at long last asked to compete to design a bank's new headquarters building. For years, the bank had been a client but actually may have thought it had been served by a firm of only one or two people, since that's all the bank ever needed for its design-related work.

Bankers used to dress conservatively, almost uniformly. But people in a design firm rarely dress that way, even when there is a dress code. Getting the team ready for the presentation, I realized that all its efforts could be cancelled in the first seconds of the encounter, if the all-principal, all-male team showed up in its usual costume.

I could count only on the lead marketing partner to dress the part. At the end of the final rehearsal, therefore, I spoke to them all about their haircuts as well as the cut of their clothing. The next morning I had seven spit-spot guys, all in gray suits with pinstripes of varying widths. And all (I am not making this up) sported shirts and ties with mauve as the featured color—just to prove, I guess, that they could dress like bankers but remain design professionals at heart.

Rabelais could say that "the habit does not make the monk," but in another case, the *car* made the man. One architect claims that no one ever took him seriously until he bought his first Mercedes. It was black—a used car, he confessed to me, but who knew?

Did the first impression created by that elegant car make the difference? I'm sure that it affected the way he felt about and conducted himself. I'm not going to argue with his success: 200 people in his office and a choice of elegant black vehicles in his garage.

And finally, here's a brief tale about how an entry lobby created a very different first impression from the one expected. A
four-letter giant firm had its entry foyer elegantly landscaped
and furnished. Plexiglas panels, suspended over a small garden,
tastefully listed all the firm's design awards—which had
stopped, curiously enough, five years before.

"What happened?" I asked. "Nothing," replied the principal
who was showing me around, genuinely surprised at my obser-
vation. "We just don't have the time to keep updating the panels." I suggested the firm might take them down, rather than
create the inevitable impression that its design group had
jumped ship five years back.

PRINCIPLE 12

Just do it

Whenever I speak at a professional gathering or in-house training session, inevitably someone will ask about the difference between marketing and selling, or public relations, publicity, and advertising. If they're into recent "hot" phrases in the communications world, they ask about "branding" and "integrated marketing communications," or IMC.

But the harder I work at providing formal definitions, the less audiences seem willing to grasp their meaning. In fact, most people seem to turn rigid on hearing formal definitions relating to marketing and public relations—even as they write down every word. How can the definitions be useful if they don't also call to action?

People want something that works for them, that gets them going in the right direction. So now I give an informal response, with a few for-instances that drive home the meaning. My final instructions are to forget the formalities and apply Nike's famous tagline, "Just do it!"

Here are a few of these definitions with anecdotes to match:

Marketing is basically anything you do to get your firm in the path of work that's right for it. Marketing requires understanding what kind of work you want to do, learning who is interested in that kind of work, deciding where you want to do that work, and assessing how prepared you are to deliver the necessary services, to what level of quality, and for what kind of fee.

Marketing is anticipatory. It entails recognizing the specifics of a client's goals and anxieties and considers how you uniquely might help address or allay them. It expects you to learn as much as you can about the organizations that interest you, and to match your services to what appears to be their need. Marketing forces you to track the world in which your current and former clients operate, to see what has changed and where you might fit in that changing equation.

Marketing—an attitude as much as a chain of actions—starts the moment an entity opens its door for business, and never ends, even after an assignment is won, even from an ongoing client. It asks if you are viable in your marketplace, and if no short list will dare ignore you—even as situations in that marketplace change.

To some firms, the very concept of "marketing" is daunting—in which case I suggest they call it "exploring." I encourage them to go on a Year of Discovery, to explore the world around them and their place in it. The assignment is to ask all the clients they have and want to have, "How and why is your work different now from what you were doing two years ago?"—and then to keep asking the question until they get to an answer that makes sense to them and makes opportunities for them. This brief, simple definition brings them right up to the marketing gates.

Selling goes to the heart of the situation. Selling includes the direct contact between your organization and a prospective client, once specific work has been identified.

Still, you can only sell people what they want to buy. Too many firms in this industry sell all the time; hard on them, hard on the prospective client: "Got work for us? We've got the muscle."

A client's top concern is that you won't understand his or her business. But if selling is all about *you*, what *you* want someone to do, about the ideas *you* feel clients should use, you are really shouting that you know more about their affairs than they do. Any textbook on client relations will tell you that the focus should be on *them*. By listening to your clients and prospects, ultimately you will learn something useful about them that will help you to make your sales pitch more compelling and make your sale.

Public relations creates a climate of acceptance for your services and work. With hundreds of techniques and tools in the communications arsenal at their disposal, public relations professionals can provide three key things: visibility, credibility, and access to the desired client.

Just as not all brandy is cognac, not all public relations is *publicity*—a prevalent confusion. Publicity entails getting coverage in the media: print, electronic, and radio/TV. What differentiates professional service firms is often too subtle for deadline-driven, mainstream publications to report to their readers—unless there is some inherent business opportunity, scandal, or personality involved.

Admittedly, it is very hard to explain to the general press what a design professional does: why, for example, tilt-up concrete panels are being used or how a change in the zoning ordinance will alter the city's profile. Years back, when computer-aided design (CAD) was getting started, we were hired to promote the one trade show then focused on this new technology. A reporter who asked me if I could show him a house that had been designed on CAD, expecting that it would look different, was disappointed when I explained it would look the same as one designed conventionally.

Before the events of 9/11 launched the reconsideration of Lower Manhattan and urban design became a blood sport, the New York City component of the American Planning Association (APA) hosted a panel of major journalists. The audience was openly—but also hostilely—seeking to learn from the panel why urban design and planning weren't covered at all in the media, ignoring that the slow process and forever build-out would bore today's high-speed news consumer. The journalists were openly annoyed at the audience's naiveté.

Actually, a successful public relations program today does not rely on publicity—and may, in fact, avoid it entirely. There are so many more things that can be done. The following list includes some options:

Ad campaigns
Advocacy
Announcements
Articles
Association leadership
Awards submissions
Book writing
Brochures and flyers
Building and neighborhood tours
Case studies
CEO coaching
Community relations
Direct mail
E-mail campaigns

Employee communications

Events

Exhibits

Marketing communications

Media training

Monographs

News releases and alerts

Newsletters (internal, external)

Op-ed pieces

Postcards

Reprints

Special supplements

Speeches and other presentations

Surveys

Technical papers

Web sites

White papers

The United States got its start through some astute public relations, well before press releases and the Internet. Paul Revere's ride was both "imageable" and effective in getting out the word. The Boston Tea Party was one great photo opportunity. Anything that Thomas Jefferson wrote to arouse enthusiasm for the new Republic was flat-out propaganda. This perspective does not show disrespect; it indicates that you have available to you all sorts of ways to "create a climate of acceptance."

Advertising entails "renting" space in a print publication, online, or on the air. Everyone knows who paid for that interval, and they know it's you talking about you. Actually, most service companies in this sector can't afford the major advertising budgets of the product manufacturers who regularly advertise, knowing that frequency brings the point home.

If this first group of definitions isn't clear, here's a story about a circus coming to town. After pitching his big top, the owner painted and posted a large sign that announced: "Circus coming tonight!" That's *advertising*. He then strapped the sign on the flank of his elephant and paraded him through the town, delighting the townspeople. That's *promotion*. But the elephant got loose and trampled the mayor's garden! That story made the evening paper. What great *publicity!* The circus owner met with the mayor, made amends for the damage, and got the mayor to officially open the circus run that evening. Now *that's* excellent *public relations.*

Branding involves the identification of a word, phrase, concept, or even a color so completely with a company that its customers always associate those words or images with the company's products or services. Branding has not just found its way into general parlance; it has washed up on the shore of the design and construction community as well—even though it really does not apply to the the kinds of products and services this community provides.

Branding also relies on uniqueness and uniformity, what has been called a "fixed point in a moving world." A brand pertains to a product's consistent quality, as experienced by a large body of consumers. For instance, you can reliably get a Coca-Cola beverage in Russia or Senegal as easily as in Houston. But in a creative business such as design, uniformity is far more difficult, perhaps even less desirable to achieve, and clients are hard won from a small pool. Moreover, "branding" anticipates additional product lines from the same house. Few professional service firms review, improve, and extend their service offerings and locations regularly, if at all.

It could be argued that SOM, Gensler, CH2M Hill, Turner—companies with multiple offices, extensive service lines, generous marketing allotments, and long histories—have been able to extend their brands. Then what's a smaller, younger company—statistically, most of the industry—to do?

I substitute the word "reputation" for "branding." That simple vocabulary shift makes it easier to discuss a company's real "identity" and purpose with a broad range of the people entrusted with its care.

For instance, try asking those in the drafting room or the boardroom to define the firm's brand and who its brand communities are, and see if anyone can respond coherently. But ask the same people about their sense of the firm's reputation, how they have heard the firm described outside the office, or what you might need to do to shore up that reputation, and you will get a revealing, useful conversation going, followed by commitment.

In truth, the integrity of either the "brand" or "reputation" depends on the conduct of the individuals involved. If you don't have internal loyalty to your firm's reputation, then you'll never be able to position your company to gain your clients' loyalty.

Integrated marketing communications addresses the need for coherence in your marketing materials. In our complex consumer marketplace, it only takes a nanosecond to figure out whether, for example, your bank's advertising agency, branch managers, and trainers even know about each other's existence.

Similarly, when a well-meaning prospective client offers to put us in touch with its graphic design firm, already at work on the brochure or Web site, we know instantly that there will be a disconnect. The governing principle is, start with the message, not the visual concept, if you wish a coherent, exportable result.

San Francisco graphic designer Doug Akagi taught me a memorable way of communicating this: "Come to me with a problem, and I'll give you a solution. Come to me with a solution, and I've got a problem."

IMC has become important because it *is* so easy for product, price, place, and promotion to be out of sync. The design and construction industry would do well to learn the manufacturing world's simple lesson about the importance of the combined approach, of coordinating, organizationwide, how you communicate values and messages.

Most professional service firms don't have the resources to constantly monitor and update their materials so that everyone is speaking with one voice. In fact, few even consider assigning this task to one of the principals. Further, most firms will do a little of this one year, then a little of that the next—very opportunistic, very disjointed, cluttered, and inefficient.

Thus, I've seen firms with as many logos, graphic styles, and messages as they have studios, divisions, or their equivalent. If that's not sufficiently confusing, consider that many Web sites are glorious examples of the talent and interests of the graphic design firms that created them, but have little relationship to the offices that the sites represent.

The real bottom line for all these working definitions is that a firm can have excellent marketing, public relations, and management people on staff or on contract, but if the professionals themselves don't adhere to the concepts just discussed, then nothing positive will result.

If your marketing/selling/public relations/publicity/branding/reputation management/integrated marketing is to be effective, you have to stay focused, engaged, staunch, flexible, experimental. Do whatever it takes—and it takes hard work. Stick to it.

Here's how Weld Coxe and I nailed some definitions in 1981. At the very start of Capelin Communications, I won the opportunity to do a fifteenth anniversary brochure for The Coxe Group, first of the design professions' outstanding management consultants. If I did a good job, I reasoned, Weld Coxe—a gifted wordsmith and marketer turned astute management consultant—would smile on my fledgling business; but I also knew that if I failed, it would be a speedy demise.

Weld and I sat down to do the brochure. Since Weld was tight on time, we challenged ourselves to come up with the concept and write it—in a day! (That's not the story, but it's a remarkable example of single-mindedness.)

We knew that the format for the services section was key. To define The Coxe Group's service offerings, we decided to use the big words—Organization Strategies and Planning, Profitability Analysis and Financial Management, and Personnel Development and Incentive Compensation. Then Weld provided a definition in "real" English for those of us who never went to business school. Last, we followed each entry with a three-sentence case study, from statement of the problem to its resolution, so—with three choices—the reader could *really* understand what was available to him. The format worked like a charm and, incidentally, remains in use several updates later.

Tell 'em who you are

I'm nobody! Who are you?
Are you nobody, too?
Then there's a pair of us—don't tell!

Emily Dickinson, author of these familiar lines, was a recluse; her horror of being in the public eye surely occasioned the poem. Many people would prefer, like her, to live their lives below the radar. A firm's principals, however, have to be "somebody" in order to get hired, gain a client's confidence, and convince a public agency or community, the whole gamut.

The two young principals of a new, hopeful office came to see me because they needed marketing collateral. They had left the office of a Major Designer to take on their first assignment and now wanted to get more work. "How did that opportunity happen?" I asked them. "Well," they confessed, "they asked us to send them 'something' about ourselves. Time was short, and frankly we didn't have anything. So we appropriated the boilerplate of our former firm, keyboarded it, substituted our name for theirs, polished the package on our Mac, and sent it off." The Ethics Police would have a field day with this. At least these two newbies admitted it.

If you are standing in a line at, say, a wedding and the person next to you asks what you do, what do you say? "I'm the newest principal of a firm of architects, planners, and interior designers that was founded in 1963 and has 18 employees." Garrison

Keillor once described some people from Lake Wobegon: "Having a conversation with these people is like dragging an unconscious person up a cliff." Watch them rush away.

If you are in the midst of giving a new business presentation, and the prospective client asks, "And what do *you* do on this project?" is your response equally lackluster? After all, clients may hire your firm but first want to know what it's going to be like to work with you, day-in, day-out, for possibly a few years. Where's the connection, the spark? The whole competitive process comes down to that simple concern: Can we get through this together?

Whether you are in the buffet line, giving a presentation, or for that matter, on trial, you need to be ready for a one-, two-, or five-minute-long introduction—without PowerPoint support.

The shortest introduction I ever heard was given by Earl Swensson, founder of a firm in Nashville. In all ways a gentleman, he would put out his hand and say, "I'm Earl Swensson, the architect." Actually, there are no titles at ESa; the business card for professional staff only states "Architect." Internally, there's a hierarchy, but not to the outside world: "Architect" proudly suffices.

I. M. Pei contributed an editorial in *The New York Times* a few years back. The italicized bio line to describe the author—dignified, sufficient—was: "I. M. Pei is an architect." Delicious understatement.

You are nonetheless entitled to a few more words in your one-minute description of what you do:

For the presentation: "I'm your principal-in-charge. That means that all decisions, all quality control, all billing, all complaints come to me. I've done five other projects of this size, and I've met the owner's budget and schedule on four of them. I'll be happy to discuss what didn't work on the fifth job when it comes to our Q&A time, so the same problems don't come up here. I've been a licensed engineer for ten years. It would mean a lot to my office to have this chance to work with you; we've looked forward to it for many years."

For the buffet: "Did I hear you say you were from Georgia? Then you probably know the soccer stadium that was built for the Olympics. My firm did the skyboxes; actually, I was the architect in charge. Can you imagine, we toured sports facilities in five other cities so our client could see the latest developments? Are you interested in soccer, by any chance?"

These are positive descriptions, not hard sell. "I help our clients to make money" may be a true statement, but you need to be careful about who's listening and through what filters, before you use a tagline to describe yourself.

You can't even assume that your family knows what you do. How awful to have Uncle Bill give the design of his new headquarters to another firm—not because he doesn't deal with relatives in business, but because he didn't know that you do "that kind of work."

Two inches outside the design professions, no one understands what you do on a daily basis, nor appreciates your impact. At the next family gathering, try this as a topic of conversation around the table: "So what *do* you do?" (And what will *you* say, in perhaps two minutes?)

I once received a letter from financial planners whom I had been considering. Their pitch for referrals was, "We hope you can comfortably describe to your friends and colleagues what we do; if you can't, please call us."

You might try the one-two-five exercises at your next principals' meeting. Listen as your colleagues state who they are. Do they express themselves in the context of the *effect* of what they do? Is each statement congruent with the firm's stated mission?

Here's an urban story about one fellow who knew his job, but not his place in the scheme of things. Heading to a meeting, I was on the cross-town bus when it stopped for a red light. From the window, I watched a sanitation man hop off his truck and proceed to heave bags of garbage into the hopper. He hit the bar to activate the jaws; observed that the scoop had broken one of the bags, spewing debris all over the street; climbed back onto his side perch; and signaled to the garbage truck's driver to proceed on their route.

I wondered: What does he consider his job? To haul X bags of garbage into the truck? Keep the truck on its schedule? Or help keep the city clean? Certainly not the latter, although I'll bet the sanitation commissioner would say differently.

To return to the theme: If you know what your work is intended to achieve—for the firm, its clients, the profession, the industry, the community, your career—it's not hard to describe to others what you do in a way that will interest them.

In one of my favorite *New Yorker* cartoons, a pack of wolves stands on a bluff, howling at a wonderful full moon. At the rear of the pack, one wolf turns to another and says, "My question is: Are we making an impact?"

PRINCIPLE 14

Therefore is the most important word in marketing

My high school put heavy emphasis on writing. Seniors were required to write an endless stream of papers, to high standards. Notwithstanding this last, grinding year of college preparation, this story is a tribute to my senior-year English teacher.

Frances Bartlett drilled into us how to write. I was considered one of the better writers in the school, if only by virtue of my position as feature editor of the school newspaper; still, I was summoned to Mrs. Bartlett's house one Saturday because I had so thoroughly not gotten her message and method.

This is what Mrs. Bartlett taught me: *Not* the old, hackneyed "tell them what you are going to tell them, tell them what you have to tell them," and so forth. Rather, "You go to the window. You open the window. Tell them *what you can now see through the open window.*"

Revolution! In other words, tell them the consequence of your actions. Tell them what's on the horizon. Tell them what you've found.

Apply the Bartlett Approach to what's wrong with marketing communications in the design and construction industry: Most brochures, Web sites, boilerplate, presentations, whatever, are static. They offer data, not insight. They say where you've been, not where you're going, and are focused on the writer or speaker, not on the reader or listener.

From your own experience reading and listening to lectures, radio, or television, you know that the only true filter is,

"What's in it for me?" Well, what's in it for your audience? What do you want them to know about your project or do with your information?

Instead, this is the kind of statement that your clients read daily: "We are a multi-disciplinary firm of thirty-five professionals and support staff, including five partners, that has been in business from the same location for fifteen years." *Yawn.*

Or: "We are a firm of 150 environmental engineers. We operate nationally without a titular headquarters, and we are proud to have been of service to our country and clients for sixty-five years." *God bless.*

Or: "We are a 'green' firm, LEED-accredited and ready to design sustainably for you." *Why should I bother?*

What is missing? The word "therefore."

Hearing this litany, the prospective client wonders: What is there in this information that matters to *me*? Does this mean they have enough people to do our job? Would all the people from these various disciplines be working on the project? Do I need all of them? And what effect will that have on project costs? What impact will the firm's "green" philosophy have on the project budget? If they've been in business for so long, is the founding generation in charge? Will we ever see any of these senior professionals once the job starts—or will we be dealing with a new generation of owners? And how seasoned are they?

Prospective clients and the larger community in which your firm operates deserve to understand where you fit in their world. They need to know the benefits accruing from your involvement.

"Therefore" will bridge your information and your actions, the problem and your solution, your promise and your follow-through. "Therefore" knits client issues to your competence and assurances, to create trust. "Therefore" shows that you listen well and perform accordingly. You are more likely to persuade them to work with you if you provide your information from their standpoint—guaranteed.

"Therefore" is simple and powerful. We pushed this rhetorical approach to the limit a few years back for EDAW, a national firm of then-150 (now, 1,100) land-use planners and designers headquartered in San Francisco. (And now you might well be asking, "Therefore?")

EDAW had been our client for a number of years when it decided to create a new graphic identity, a new perspective, a new voice—and, certainly, a new brochure system written from the point of view of the recipient, not the provider. We gained permission to ask twenty of EDAW's most interesting clients to be our "advisory panel." One by one, we asked them what they like to know when they receive materials from design professionals.

We also asked these advisers why they selected not just EDAW but also any of its competitors, and how. Did they get what they expected, or did the reality differ from what was promised, and how? What would they have liked to have asked during the selection process that hadn't occurred to them then, and would they select EDAW again?

Each member of this forthright group told us time and again that he or she did not care about the "national firm with X offices and X employees" boilerplate—so inert! Furthermore, each expected excellent planning and design as part of EDAW's skills package.

What each adviser wanted to know was: How would the job be done? Could he count on EDAW to be there at nine o'clock in the morning or nine o'clock in the evening for community review board sessions? Who would really work on the job? What was EDAW's track record on zoning? What would happen if a client wanted pink flamingos instead of high design? Was EDAW expensive because it was so big and therefore had overhead to cover?

After the interviews, we sought answers to the clients' questions from EDAW's principals, thereby defining their process and also the firm's soul.

The brochure that resulted was entirely cast from this dialogue: tough questions and very candid answers. As for the flamingos, with the help of Joe Brown, now EDAW's president and CEO, that answer became: "We're not in the business of giving the client a flat 'no,' though we've been known to give a flat 'yes.' It's our responsibility to . . . explore ways to meet your objectives. If pink flamingos are the answer, you'll get the best pink flamingos we can deliver." What an exceptional mission statement!

This took time, clear heads, and commitment—but as a result, EDAW transformed the way it talked about itself and marketed its services. The brochure was effective because it announced: *Here's what we are and here's how that prepares us to work with and for you. Are we a good match?* Either a prospective client liked the direct answers and memorable style of the firm expressed by the brochure, or it didn't. The brochure actually helped clients decide whether they would enjoy working with EDAW. That's high-performance language.

PRINCIPLE 15

1 + 1 equals 11

So It Was Just a Simple Wedding, Sara Kasdan's hilarious novel from the 1960s, has been reissued; now *that's* durability in the usually throwaway publishing industry. In the book, the mother and father of the bride decided that the wedding should be held in their lovely home—except that, by the time the wedding occurred, everything in the house had been rebuilt, rearranged, and redecorated. The book's message rings true: there is no such thing as a simple wedding.

Let me add my own corollaries: *Nothing* is ever simple. And, because people *do* care about how they are perceived, there is nothing like having to prepare for an event (a speech, client visit, or presentation) or write for publication to motivate people to sharpen the way they present themselves. There is certainly nothing "simple" about these situations; each demands the highest performance, which requires excellent thinking, excellent logistics, and excellent materials. Mies van der Rohe set the tone: "God is in the details." (Actually, historian Aby Warburg coined the phrase in the 1920s. Mies, however, used it so cogently and frequently that most people attribute it to him.)

"Simple" is clearly not part of the public relations and marketing lexicon, but that doesn't mean something should be avoided. On the contrary, anything that improves the firm's relationships with its client base merits full attention.

Here's the math involved: When Ryc Loope was brought into The Durrant Group to grow the firm into a global organization, Durrant's existing mission statement included the formula 1 + 1 > 2. Upping the ante—and putting everyone inside and outside the firm on notice—Ryc reformulated the math into an inspiring principle: 1+1 equals 11.

In the '70s, when newsletters were in their heyday—before desktop publishing made them so commonplace and mediocre that they had to go on hiatus—I explained to the principals of an A/E firm that newsletters had unforeseen benefits. After all, that much money could not be spent without demanding to know what would be the return on the investment—so lo! the firm's marketing goals, or at least the marketing goals for the publication, were defined.

Then, because the newsletter required a masthead, all the related graphics—logo, colors, typeface, cover note letterhead—were reconsidered, coordinated, and tightened up. Because good visuals were essential, a shoot that couldn't occur until the last light fixture was in place or until perhaps cash flow improved was amazingly scheduled "for the newsletter." Because articles were needed that would put the spotlight on both the client and the firm, the firm's professionals had to convey what they had learned in the course of doing something for that client, project, or location.

After a while, the newsletter took on a life of its own—to the point that I would hear, "Are we going to need this photographed so it can appear in the fall newsletter?" Or a branch office or specialty service group would complain that it hadn't gotten equal visibility to another unit, that it needed materials to promote its services, and what was going to be done about *that?*

Not surprisingly, all these preparations served the marketing efforts very well. The newsletter provided a way to be regularly in touch with clients, prospective clients, and friends of the firm. Visuals for presentations became readily available. Research for the articles yielded information to heighten the significance of the work. Moreover, the people who developed business for the firm had an abundance of anecdotes and language to enliven their outreach. Not bad for a supposedly simple newsletter.

How does "1+1 equals 11" pertain to an event? We recently helped a firm organize a series of informal lunches for its current and former clients. The purpose was to introduce the next generation of principals to the client's parallel next generation of executives, to learn firsthand what was going on in the client's realm, and to explore ways that creative design professionals could help smart clients to advance their own goals.

Shades of *Simple Wedding*, the first reaction of the architects involved, when they heard our idea, was to shoot it down. They indicated that the firm's main conference room was entirely unsuitable for this purpose, ill lit, in need of fresh paint, several generations behind in technology, unwindowed, and not large enough. No one had ever voiced these comments before.

Undeterred—after updating the lighting track and cleaning the carpet and upholstery—the tenacious director of marketing set up a couple of catered but otherwise informal lunches in the office with a few former and friendly clients, and got an excellent result, including restoring one of the "lost" client relationships.

The director also held a more formal luncheon in a private club and again included members of the successor generation. This event brought together a group of clients from a specific sector to discuss the effect of the current economic climate on construction projects in *their* industry—each would hear how other organizations similar to theirs were persevering in an era of constraints. This, too, was effective, but the final decision was that, for the hosting firm, the club approach was too formal and too costly to repeat regularly.

What was achieved? First and foremost, the firm's next-generation leaders gained confidence along with access. At the same time, the principals were obliged to update their lists of key current, prospective, and past clients to see which companies, locations, and sectors could yield new opportunities. The briefing packet prepared for the firm's guests yielded insights, as well as questions the architects could ask clients about how they see the next few years. The marketing group also had an excellent reason to create a package to introduce the new generation of principals.

Another galvanizing event is a presentation—perhaps a speech at a conference or university, a client's office, or your own office. What's important is that the event be memorable. A good stand-up presentation requires visuals—excellent new or archival photographs, and quality, cleaned-up artwork, including drawings—as well as definitive facts and figures and failure-proof equipment. Most important, the speaker needs to thoughtfully consider what he or she knows. And that's before a word goes down on paper.

Creating a presentation—learning the topic as well as rehearsing the text—sharpens public speaking skills. I also suggest that the speaker, not the convener, write the introduction, to achieve the right tone for the lead-in. Very often, a graphic designer skilled in, say, PowerPoint presentations becomes part of the team—an important resource to have available and indoctrinated in the firm's ways. If the speaker is leading or participating in a panel, the additional connections will extend thinking about the topic and expand the firm's network.

Traveling a distance to make a "simple" presentation poses other opportunities. Speakers who fly in that morning and fly out again the moment they have finished speaking do not help themselves. Whom do you know or want to know in that location? Can you tour area projects that are similar to ones your firm is doing, or wants to do? Who might be coming to the conference that you would like to have in your own audience? What colleague from a professional association could you call on? Why hightail it out of town, when there could be a full schedule of new business calls, client development events, and other opportunities to meet people, all of which could help you develop your business?

Thus any "simple" activity can yield insight, opportunity, and marketing materials that will continue to prove useful. For instance, amortize your efforts by giving the same talk to a private, perhaps all-client audience, an allied association closer to home, a city agency related to your firm's work, or perhaps an editorial group. You might even try it out on the people in your office, the most candid of any audience, enriching their knowledge of a topic important to you and your firm and inspiring them to do the same. Each situation yields new insights, new confidence, and a proportionately lower cost of development. As Louis Pasteur said, "Chance favors the prepared mind."

PRINCIPLE 16

Nothing of value is free

When my mother rounded the last bend at the end of her life, she developed one quirk that was particularly liberating: She decided to stop paying bills. "Uh, Mother, the electric company gets sticky about that," I would say. And she would answer, "I've paid enough bills in my life." Rip. Rip.

It was easy enough to get around this little problem with my mother, but how often has a client of yours just decided not to acknowledge your bills or pay you? Or, you've hesitated to ask for additional money that you earned by providing additional services that were requested? Or, shoe on the other foot, how many times have you not paid subconsultants because cash was short—but avoided discussing the problem along with not paying?

Years back I was struck—"terrified" is more accurate—by a chart I saw when I first started my business; it illustrated that the longer you go without being paid, the less you will be paid, if at all. So I have been especially alert to the payment issue, all around. Why *do* people have such trouble talking about money, or asking for it?

One environmental graphics designer admits that his firm's work doesn't appear until almost the end of the project, and that he is, therefore, toward the end of the payment line. When money tightens at the end of a job, he knows who will really feel the pinch. How do you handle that, I wondered? "Gently. Calmly. We just keep asking, and our voice is never raised. Very few people are really dishonest," he believes. "If cash flow is the issue, I ask the client how much he can pay each month? Even if it's 500 dollars, at least we're slowly getting paid."

One professional firm with multiple offices values client relationships but insists on being paid, no matter what. The principals have a soft-voiced woman in their distant administrative headquarters staff call the delinquent client. Without coercion, she finds the person responsible for nonpayment, ferrets out the issue, and arranges a payout. This indirect approach saves face and brings in far more payment than roughhousing would net.

When one of our clients is experiencing difficulty paying us, we move quickly to remedy the situation. "Whose money is it anyway?" asked an "Entrepreneur's Byline" column in *BusinessWeek Online*. "Tolerate uncollected debts and you might as well be giving your customers no-interest loans."

There may be extenuating circumstances you want to consider, but the point is well taken. Ask yourself, Why *am* I in business? Negative cash positions benefit no one, since you become unable to deliver essential services.

My second question of a nonpaying client is, How are you communicating this cash crunch to other firms to whom you are obligated? My usual counsel is that it would be a great deal easier—not to mention honorable—to simply initiate the conversation when money is tight, obtain permission to slow down payment, or, ultimately, offer a payment schedule or settlement.

If you are the one who owes the money, the very fact that you have taken the first step diffuses much of the hostility toward you and restores goodwill, if not service. It bespeaks professionalism. Let's hear Mark Twain on this: "Always do right. This will gratify some people and astonish the rest."

As for the principle that "nothing of value is free," which comes from Ayn Rand, here's an anecdote about how to get paid what you're worth. One architect/principal to whom I've consulted is exceptionally adept at negotiating for his company. If his client attempts to lower his fee as negotiations proceed, he smiles and raises it. The frustrated client demands an even lower fee, and the undaunted principal raises it even higher. Hardball? Guess who gets the fee he wants?

I learned early on not to drop fees to get a project, no matter how much I want it. We got our very second contract by reminding our prospective client that no one knew better than his office that price should not be a factor in selection. Then I removed any competitive edge by charging one dollar less than the lowest acceptable bid. (Such moxie! We could barely afford pencils.) We got their blessing to proceed, and they got a great brochure for a ridiculous price. Chalk it up to experience, but I learned to be aware that competitors lowball.

Communicating your worth is a skill truly worth learning. If your client requests work beyond the contract, nothing is so time-pressured that you can't advise him about the cost and then whip out your standard contract extension form for him to sign. It's a very ordinary procedure. If you don't get your form back immediately, you probably were not going to be paid, and you shouldn't have started anyhow. Plus, if you don't request additional fees when your client requests the service, then what are your chances of recovering that money when the job is over?

The most important letter of all is the service professional's calm warning to the well-served but nonpaying client. In today's economic environment, some companies deny ever having received the bill. Yet jewelers send precious gems through regular mail, and it's funny how those packages don't go astray.

Unless the client has a real objection to your invoice, write him to ask what is holding up payment. Since you are already one step closer to a court of law—or court of public opinion, whichever governs in your community—you must go unapologetically on record. The first, all-business letter simply states that apparently the attached invoice has been overlooked and should be honored immediately. The second letter says that your designated person will be calling to understand the problem.

It's always a good idea for your chief financial officer to know the client's financial team members on a first-name basis, because at some point you will need to get to the people who authorize and actually pay the bill. If the problem is that your client's project manager hasn't even signed off, then that person needs to be handled tactfully but firmly.

Put your comptroller or chief bookkeeper on the case from the get-go. A letter to a new client is worth considering: "Welcome to ABC Engineers' client family. I wanted to introduce myself to you: I'm the one who develops the invoices. We would like to be sure that our invoices match your process and requirements, so I'll give you a call. May I come by next week?"

A letter like that—copied to the principal-in-charge, project manager, and, with the new client's permission, the comptroller's counterpart—paves the way to prompt payment, encourages speedy resolution of disputes (easier among "friends"), or, at the least, flags payment problems.

As for raising fees, why not? If you are careful about timing the increase, if your increase is reasonable, if you give advance notice, if you are providing better technology that accelerates the project or makes it more fail-safe, or if you haven't raised fees in two years, again, why not? This hard-working, long-hours industry needs to raise its self-image, and money is as good a starting place as any.

Many years ago, a prospective client challenged me during the final interview because his firm's hourly rates were lower than ours. Since we were nowhere near the hourly rate of his lawyer or accountant, I calmly responded that he needed a wake-up call about the value of our professional services—and his. "The first assignment is for us to help you get your fees up to where they should be," I told him. "You're letting your clients take advantage of you." He was clearly not used to being talked to so directly.

The French have a great saying: *Si tu aimes le miel, ne crains pas les abeilles.* Translation: "If you like honey, you can't be afraid of bees."

Shoot to where the duck is going

The mood in our client's conference room quickly became tense. The purpose of the meeting was to discuss the first draft of the firm's marketing plan, the first official one in its history. Now that a new generation of principals had been named, it should have been an active, optimistic moment.

But the marketing plan, to which each principal and the marketing director had contributed, wasn't a plan. Instead, it was a list of ongoing sales opportunities and assignments. No vision, no research, no timetables, no champions for a sector, or even someone willing to gather and combine this information into an actual plan.

What happened? Each of the six people around the table had come with his or her working definition of "marketing" and even "marketing plan." None of them knew the others' definitions. And, as we found out during a testy hour and a half, neither did they agree with their colleagues' characterizations. For want of a common definition, the marketing plan was lost.

Francis Ford Coppola believes that the difference between making a good movie and making a bad movie is getting everyone involved in making the *same* movie. It would have been nice if those folks around the table had felt likewise about their marketing plan.

You don't need to create a plan that is so big it preoccupies the marketing group for a month and sends the partners into spasms. You need to create a great vision of what the firm wants to achieve in the coming year(s), and bring it down to real time, having assessed the situation and the available information. One of my colleagues, James Lukaszewski, describes it as going to the edge of the horizon, picking out something, and talking about how to get there.

What's too often missing in planning isn't the discipline; it's the energy and interest to move ahead and the ability to articulate and communicate the vision. It shouldn't be boring; if anything, it should lift those who find the firm a tad dull right out of their comfortable chairs.

A number of years ago, I created a daylong program in New York for the design and building community titled "How to Finish Your Marketing Plan." Having read the same business publications, almost everyone had started and then shelved his or her firm's marketing and business plans. What kind of leadership doesn't plan for the future?

To guarantee that people would have all the skills and information needed to get back to their planning, we had brought in a strong group of lecturers, including Laurin McCracken, for the planning process. Laurin, who is now the strategies officer at Looney Ricks Kiss, was batting in the cleanup spot. He earned a lot of friends that day by giving them the simplest of instructions: List the ten entities for which you want to design or build. And then he showed them how to go on the attack just for this high-yield group. People couldn't wait to get back to their offices to give Laurin's approach a shot. But what he really did was empower them to imagine a more enticing future for themselves and their firm. They could go anywhere on that fuel.

Perhaps there are three additional lists: those ten clients you want to keep, those ten that have left the fold that you want back, and those few to which you can turn if the bottom falls out. Each needs its own strategy, objectives, and time frames.

Here are a few other ways to update and energize your planning process and also to make it more productive:

If your plan isn't realistic, you'll get discouraged and waste a lot of time and money. Better to get started on something manageable, and then next year, exchange your plan for a larger size.

Instead of fighting for a bigger piece of the pie, make a bigger pie. Everyone will benefit.

Fund the plan sufficiently so you *can* get there. If you don't have enough budget, then go after fewer opportunities, or share the costs with the other offices on your team.

Permit yourself to bail out when you feel that you have done everything you can and it's not working. Or replace the market champion, if the person you selected has underperformed. However, if a prospective organization has been giving you a runaround, don't hesitate to go back one last time and ask the client what didn't work, or if there is someone else, in another division or a step up the ladder, who might be responsive?

Make certain that all your references are good ones, so you can proceed with confidence. Each time we've done an audit to assess how a firm is perceived in its marketplace, some former or even current client surprisingly turns out to be annoyed or worse about the people we are representing. How could the firm not know that this would be a hostile conversation? Better to stay in touch! Better yet, tour the building you've designed or built to see how it is holding up—and, at the same time, learn how the relationship is holding up, as well. This would absolutely not be a sales call, and it would be difficult to charge for it, although an opportunity might surface.

"What gets measured, gets done" is a time-tested business principle. What quantifiable performance standards does your firm set for marketing? Louis Gerstner, Jr., the former chairman of the board of IBM Corporation, is often quoted as saying, "Never confuse activity with results." Assign someone the responsibility, the time, and the resources to complete the work of the plan—and hold him or her accountable for making it happen.

While writing this book, I often had lunch delivered to my desk from the local Chinese restaurant. One fortune cookie provided the ultimate planning wisdom: "Many a false step is made by standing still."

PRINCIPLE 18

Control spin

Logically, people want to see their name—and also their firm's name—in print. That's a very American thing. But in this industry, is that desire realistic? Worth the risk involved?

What's the risk? That your story won't get picked up, thereby squandering an opportunity and wasting your firm's time and money? That's only one peril; I'll address others further along.

First, what's the reward? One architect, a ravenous publicity hound, approached my firm years ago, insisting that he needed (deserved!) exceptional publicity so that, in a fee negotiation, "They wouldn't dare drop my fee. I'll be famous!"

This anecdote is not an endorsement of his approach. especially since he wanted us to arrange for someone to scale the exterior of his Manhattan office tower to get to his new office's open house—thereby attracting police and photographers and assuring coverage in the tabloids. I think not, I told him, although he did have a point about the negotiation posture.

Still, seeking news coverage is a helpful exercise on its own. To achieve increased awareness of your name, talent, and approach, you must be clear, articulate, confident, well documented, and communicative. You have to prepare if you want to get into print or on the air or the Internet. You must know your audiences and what resonates with them. All of the preparation is excellent for your firm.

Where then are the hazards? First, much of what happens in the design industry is process; it takes years, not sound bites. Most projects don't inspire Ground Zero passions. The *American Journalism Review* recently pointed out that current journalism is event-oriented and thrives on controversy, but it is not so good at reporting on what evolves. "They would cover the crucifixion and miss Christianity," a pundit explained.

Second, according to *Washington Post* columnist William Raspberry, although it's clear on the sports pages that the reporters want the home team to win, "the reporters in the rest of the paper don't appear to want our cities and country to succeed." Yet the work of anyone in the design and construction industry is geared to improving places and lives in myriad ways. That's often not on the reporters' wavelength.

Third, the press isn't exactly waiting for your news. Kristen Richards, who founded and edits the daily digest, ArchNewsNow.com, admits she has a WIGATI file: when I get around to it. Major editors receive dozens of releases a day in the mail and many more electronically. I once sat in the office of a *Fortune* editor while the mountain of mail in his inbox tilted and cascaded onto the floor. Fine with him, he laughed; he wasn't going to have the time to read it all, anyhow.

Further, it's a myth that writers in the media will do the research so they can write fairly and completely. They candidly will tell you that they don't have the time, the backup staff, or even the equipment to do it—not to mention the inside knowledge or a sense, at times, to know that something is missing. Even our own press may neglect to check with associated firms or the client, to see who really has met the challenges described, and how.

More from Kristen Richards, interviewed by Sam Hall Kaplan for *City Observed*, his NPR/Los Angeles program: "Few [editors] ever get to actually walk through the projects they write about, let alone talk to any end-users. Most have to rely on images the architects and/or clients choose to show, well-honed press releases, sound bites from press conferences, and, if lucky, a five-minute phone interview with the architects."

Gordon Wright, the long-standing voice of *Building Design & Construction*, described to me how the "meticulous coordination" of his trip to participate in an SMPS panel resulted in one excellent experience: "An architecture firm's marketing person presented me with an itinerary that covered the evening of my arrival and the following day. She set up tours of two projects with which her firm was not involved, as well as one project her firm had designed. Her itinerary was complete with details such as 'remove luggage' when I transferred from one person's car to someone else's. She accommodated her schedule to meet my transportation needs."

Result: "Needless to say," he concluded, "because of these actions above and beyond the call of duty, I won't soon forget her firm."

Architectural Record's Robert Ivy told me, "Nothing beats good work. Great work stands on its own merits, particularly if attached to a known quantity. On the other hand, people not as well known or going into a more ambitious arena require explanation and presentation." He remembers receiving from my office the package on Monona Terrace, the building that Frank Lloyd Wright originally designed in 1938 for a Wisconsin lakefront site. It was finally completed as a conference and exhibition center by Tony Puttnam of Taliesin Architects. This was the eighth round of designs, nearly forty years after Wright's death. "We wouldn't have taken it so seriously if there hadn't been such a thorough presentation," he commented. "Monona Terrace decidedly required an explanation, a careful description, and historical context. If it weren't Wright, it would have been easy to dismiss."

Result: "Is Monona Terrace Really Wright?" March 1998.

C. C. Sullivan, editor-in-chief of *Architecture*, relates his worst experience, which had to do with unspoken expectations: "[An engineer] was supposed to provide background, drawings, and other technical information, and the opportunity to interview his staff. Internally, he apparently represented this upcoming article as a vehicle to publicize the engineers and his firm's glorious history. The situation devolved into a 'Mexican stand-off,' where he would not release any of the materials or authorize interviews without assurances regarding what would be published and how. While this may be a common situation, his increasingly belligerent attitude and hardball tactics added a touch of the surreal to our dealings."

Result: "Of course, the opportunity was lost—for both of us."

Here are some key points to remember when you seek to be published:

Know what you want to say, have the content to back it up, and stay on message. General Tommy Franks's daily press briefings from Iraq were memorable not so much because he calmly and generously answered every question he was asked, but because he gave people the answers *he* wanted people to hear.

Focus on the constituencies you want to reach. It should be clear which high-impact publications to target: for starters, the ones your clients read, followed by those that relate to the users. Art Gensler confides that for every design publication he reads, he reads two magazines that his clients read.

Become a reliable and available source for journalists. If you don't have a good story to share with the media, you can always propose a story about someone or something that you aren't working on. Rather, share background, provide access to people, indicate developments, and comment on current events about which you are informed but not involved. As C. C. Sullivan points out, "Individuals don't realize that their personal perspectives and experiences allow them to identify emerging trends, key issues, and surprising phenomena."

Be prepared. Back up your query with a news release, fact sheet (our basic form is six pages, before it is filled in), a design or approach statement that tells the story of the project (why? how? opportunities/constraints?), biographies of key people, and at least preliminary visuals.

Treat journalists as real people. They aren't traveling incognito. They have their preconceptions and misconceptions, however. And it's still their game, ball, court, and rules. They have the right to decide whether they'll let you play.

The year he was president of the Professional Services Management Association, I took Ed Vick on a media tour. Ed is an exceptional engineer, founder of Kimley-Horn, and an outstanding "people person." We gave him recent articles by the journalists he was meeting, so he could prepare. "I have to tell you," he confessed to one editor as a meeting began, "your article on the Tower of Pisa was one of the best explanations I've ever read." You can imagine how well that interview went.

Play the tape to the end. Before the interview starts, consider how you want it to come out and keep working toward that goal. One usually courteous and measured architect invited to dinner an editor-in-chief whom he really hoped would cover a project his architecture firm had designed. Over dinner, though, the architect vehemently challenged many of the opinions that the editor voiced. "I'm not very good at this," he later admitted to me, after serious damage was done.

Reporting, like any design, can be decoded. Buy three competing publications and see how each covers the same story. Listen to Barbara Walters, Larry King, and Charlie Rose (who often interviews architects) for the methods they use to draw out the source and secrets. Described as having the "fastest hearing" in the business, Rose drawls "Because . . . ?" as he looks intently at you, then waits enrapt for your response. One of the great Walters questions: "What do you think is the greatest misconception about you?" *Achtung!*

Be careful about what you wish for. An excellent firm of urban designers asked us to get them into *The Wall Street Journal.* Duany Plater-Zyberk & Company had recently made the front page. "How important is this to you?" I asked. "Very." Before we proceeded, we took the DPZ article apart, extracting the pointed questions the *Journal* must have asked about its business. When we presented that list to our clients to get them prepared, they were horrified; they would never reveal such details about their own firm, they declared.

Even the local business publications are not benign. Many people want to be in one of the *Crain's* local publications.

Crain's, however, has a "but" paragraph that people don't spot until it hits them. The format is: Paragraph 1—Aren't they great? Paragraph 2—Things appear to be going so well for them. Paragraph 3+—Hold on! There are storm clouds approaching fast. Final two paragraphs—Then again . . . .

Treat the press as gingerly as you would a client. Although we always expect professional journalists to be accurate, facts can elude them. It can be frustrating to see an error appear and become codified, by dint of publication.

In the course of an assignment for a firm of interior architects, we managed to catch the attention of the architecture critic of *The New York Times*, who wrote a favorable piece—but omitted the firm's name! While I can't overstate the extent of the mistake (the paper printed a correction the next day, but so what?), the blistering letter that our client sent to the chagrined critic was equally indefensible. What did it achieve?

On the other hand, when something good does happen—the comments are mostly favorable, the color of the photography in print is reasonably close to reality, the names are spelled correctly, the owner is quoted saying something pleasant—a thank-you letter should be automatic and instantaneous. Journalists work very hard but receive few thank-you letters—and how well they remember them!

This chapter has been all about dealing with the media, and, yes, it can be done well. Yet a red flag appears before my eyes if we, in my office, are described as "publicists." Here's why: I immediately understand that what we do and bring to the assignment has *not* been understood. And if a client or potential client, or the media, itself, does not understand what we do, that's a problem.

Publicists usually report on what has happened; their stories are conceived with distinct parameters. Publicists let the world know where an organization or individual has been, and is, up until now. We, on the other hand, take the approach of anticipating where an organization or individual will be heading, and then we tell the story from that perspective. Thus, our real work is to help the media to see that future, too.

The whole purpose of getting your firm in the media is to gain visibility so that like-minded people can find and link up with you. That's why content, as well as forward thrust, is so important. Of course, a firm deserves credit for a job well done, a thought well conceived, a project well activated. But where is it heading with this? What is around the bend for the organization and those around it? *That's* what it should be considering.

PRINCIPLE 19

Everyone *owns* the client

What is the *experience* of working with your firm? The answer is worth knowing. We are a nation geared to experiences—travel, shopping, and ceremonies. Even your neighborhood restaurant has to provide an "experience." In my city, even the coffee shops strive aggressively to recall the diners of the '50s.

At some point, everyone in your firm will have direct contact with at least some of your clients, colleagues, consultants, friends of the firm, the press, and vendors. What do your employees say to these outsiders? What do these outsiders then say about your firm to others?

More to the point, what happens when someone on the outside wants to speak to someone in the firm, perhaps to you? Suppose a blind request for information comes into your office. As legend has it, a Japanese firm called to request information from three American architecture firms. At RTKL, the message went instantly to then-Chairman Harold Adams, who answered immediately, while the other two offices delayed. That blind call and turnaround response began RTKL's golden reputation and involvement in Japan—thanks to a well-trained receptionist and marketing group that cared about an unknown caller who might become a client.

What happens when a known client or other important person calls you or sends you an e-mail, and you are away from your office at that moment or week? Does the message get swallowed up in your voice-mail system? Who monitors your voice mail? Does the person at the switchboard track down your assistant and make sure that the message is delivered and the urgency to act understood? Do you have a system that allows an alternate principal to automatically take a client's call when the principal-in-charge is away, ensuring that the client can always reach someone in authority who can speak about his job and who values the relationship?

It surprises me that some professional service firms greet telephone calls electronically, obliging outside callers to go through a menu and leave a message without once talking to a human being. This is a *service* industry. Even if your phone operator—we applaud the firm that calls that job "Director of First Impressions"—provides the caller with the option to leave a message there or on voice mail, at least someone cares that you get that call or message.

Joe Coates, a D.C.-based futurist, told a PSMA audience an anecdote about when he called a firm after-hours. He reached a manager, who admitted that he didn't know how to transfer the call, but if Joe would call back, he could leave a message at the switchboard by immediately hitting "0." Joe's reaction: "That firm hires damn fools."

DesignIntelligence featured an article that began with the warning: "Your presentation is beautiful, your Web site works, but your receptionist is a bear." In one case, I called a client and got the regular person at the front desk. She sounded as if mayhem had broken out and the police had surrounded the place. "What's wrong?" I asked, very concerned. "The phones," she wailed, barely breathing, "haven't stopped ringing all morning."

"Uh, isn't that good news?" I asked. Clearly, not to her. She was replaced.

Another receptionist we've experienced received our packages, usually sent to someone working with us on deadline, placed these important materials in what we came to call the "Sacred Closet," and never told the intended recipient— expecting that person to discover the delivery had been made. We began calling and e-mailing the ultimate recipient when packages were in motion.

Yet another receptionist never bothered to tell us that the person whom we really needed to reach for an immediate newspaper interview was away from the office, let alone for how long. We learned this after several unreturned calls—and after the reporter's deadline had passed.

In public relations, if you don't know something, the automatic response you are trained to give is, "I will find out and get right back to you." Even if you are having trouble finding the answer, still you get back to the caller and give a new estimated time. When the situation entails dealing with an editor on deadline, this follow-up is essential.

If you think this problem only concerns the front desk, you may not be aware that a skilled investigative journalist can crack any firm's phone number sequence and get through— even to a sequestered team. Here's the scenario we used to alert and then train an entire Superfund team:

Suppose that the region's daily paper knows you have the assignment for the toxic site and even knows the contact person's name, not too hard to identify, since this is on the public record. The journalist calls the office, guessing a random number within your sequence. Someone answers, identifying himself. "Oh," says the caller, without identifying the reason for the call, "I asked the switchboard for John Smith; I'm sorry, could you transfer me?" What's the normal, courteous reaction? "Just a second, I'll do that."

As our script continued, the next person to pick up the phone was the department's administrator. The journalist blasts out: "I'm from *The Dispatch*. Two children who live right across the street from your Superfund site have just been taken to the hospital. They are deathly ill. What is your firm's comment?" What would you expect that clerk to say? "Oh, my god, that's terrible" would be understandable—and you can imagine that quote in the lead paragraph of the front-page article that evening.

Everyone in your firm needs to remember the time-honored principle: "The perception of service is almost as important as the service itself." Empower everyone in your office to make it easy for your clients to work with you. Your client's experience should be, at the very least, that he is well served.

First, you market internally

Who would argue that the most important thing you can do to obtain or retain clients is to do a good job? But client satisfaction, pride, and payment aren't the only reasons you take an assignment.

Think about the work currently in the office: Why did you seek it? Why did you get it? Where does its successful completion take the firm?

Sailors have a useful saying: "One hand for the ship, one hand for yourself." One hand holds the tiller, steering the boat to its destination; the other hand grasps the gunwale, so you are still inside the boat when you get there. In marketing terms: Every job you do—"do well" is implied—should take the firm closer to where it is heading.

There are many reasons to seek or accept a project. Cash flow is one of them. Some firms consciously have a client or category of work on which they can constantly rely for a steady stream of profitable projects to underpin the firm—a zone of financial comfort, as it were.

Other valid reasons for taking an assignment include mastering a new expertise, opening a new location for the office or a new marketplace, getting onto a desired client's insider list, giving back to your community, gaining exceptional visibility, trying out a possible merger relationship, or getting in on the ground floor of a trend. Everyone knows—or should know—that you are in business to make money. Yet these additional reasons often remain unspoken to the team responsible for the project.

Internal marketing—explaining to your own employees what the deal is and what is at stake—is crucial. It's a myth that everyone in the office knows why you won the job. Your professional and administrative employees need to understand and champion the firm's business strategies and business development.

The job description of the principal-in-charge includes communicating to employees what their piece of the whole is, how they fit into the organization—and then how the office fits into the client's picture. (Keeping this in front of the team is part of the job description and training of project managers, as well.)

Here are some of the things your employees need to know:

The mission of the project, from the client's perspective. There's a big difference between "they need more space so they bought an old building" and "they felt that, by taking over the old warehouse for their new headquarters, they could get a building at a good price and also accelerate the city's downtown revitalization." Once your employees know what's at stake, and this vision captures their creativity, they might come up with even better solutions.

The mission of the project, from your firm's perspective. What does it have to accomplish?

The promises your firm has made, and why: not just time and budget, but also level, quality, and speed of service.

The client's definition of success. Take note: The quality of the structure or space may be their given. What else is important to them? In a document from the late '90s that redefined "the client," the American Institute of Architects weighed in on this: "The client is more interested in how the facility works and supports its work processes than . . . in what the place looks like."

Why the firm won the job—and why another firm lost the opportunity. And if it's a public project, what public interest will the firm serve through its client?

What the client fears the most. In addition to wasting the client's investment, a botched project places some people's careers on the line.

How your firm plans to find out whether the client is really satisfied throughout the process. And, finally, how you are going to communicate that regularly to the team.

The institutional client base of Helpern Architects almost always requires the firm to deal with committees and, like all architecture firms, with public and agency reviews. In an article in *AIArchitect*, the weekly online publication of the AIA, President David Helpern wrote: "Gather everyone who will be involved in the project to discuss the client's culture, level of experience, personalities, and expectations; goals for the client, your firm, and the team; priorities; and details down to how to dress when you are together with the client. This will set forth responsibility, authority, and accountability right from the outset."

One advantage of this clarity is that, when it comes to evaluating the team, individual employees, and the project manager as a leader and role model, you have established real benchmarks for performance. You can afford to be intolerant.

Another advantage is that a well-briefed project team becomes an excellent public relations force for the firm. All team members know where they are heading, and why. That's golden for those who are also involved in recruiting, business development, and dealing with the media.

Relationships with repeat clients also need to be nurtured. Those clients admire, appreciate, and trust you, which is fortifying as well as profitable. It is important for the team serving a returning or evergreen client to know your expectations, even if they seem self-evident. Some firms acknowledge the person who brings in new business; those who are the stewards of long-term client relationships deserve your recognition, too.

Although the ability to communicate well is a critical skill for principals, project managers traditionally have not been made accountable for this. Yet they communicate all the time—just not necessarily well. They communicate to the firm's leadership, to the staff, and especially to the client. Certainly, the project manager is the firm's front line. Anyone who followed General Schwartzkopf's strategy in Kuwait knows that the Gulf War was won not at headquarters, but in the field with the people engaged in day-to-day battle.

Today's project managers are constantly explaining the job to people at home and in the field, speaking for the firm at meetings, writing minutes, and making presentations. Just as principals need training and regular assistance so they can speak and write effectively, we strongly urge that project managers receive the same attention.

PRINCIPLE 21

Think before you write

Too many people forget this simple mantra: Strategic thinking comes before writing. Yet many marketing departments spew out endless, aimless paragraphs as they rush ahead to produce proposals and marketing materials, including brochures, Web sites, articles, press releases, and speeches.

Friedrich Bohm of NBBJ once explained to me that in his firm, if you couldn't talk about the project coherently, you weren't yet in a position to design it. "You have to be able to get your hands around it," he insists. The same coherence pertains to a firm's marketing materials.

Let's say that your firm has done a project really well and you want to tell the world about it via the most basic of communications: the press release. Here are twenty questions to consider before you even start to write:

How will this story fit into the marketing goals of the firm?

Do we have the client's permission to tell this story?

What messages about the firm's effectiveness does the story support? For instance: Are we a design trendsetter? Technological innovator? Manager of complex projects?

What is the client's approval process, and how long will that take?

Is this the right stage in the project to get out the news?

Can we get this story out within the current window of opportunity, or is some other medium indicated by this time frame?

Can we summarize the project in a sentence that will interest someone who is not directly involved in the project? (This sentence might become your headline.)

Is there a strong visual available, and do we have permission to use it?

Who is the right spokesperson for the firm? Will that person be around when the story breaks, in case further interviewing is needed?

Can we get someone from the client side or another authority to support the project in the press release (and in interviews, if needed)?

What categories of clients, prospects, and friends within our marketplace and our community would want to know this news?

Have we explored all the print and electronic media outlets that reach these people, and is that list up-to-date?

What in our story will these *media* consider newsworthy? (Friends of the firm may rejoice at a new assignment, but will the readers of a particular magazine consider it significant and useful?)

Do we have an agreement with other members of the design and building team about credits and about who "owns" the right to tell the story first?

Do we have the budget necessary to reproduce the visuals well and mail or deliver the package?

Can this release fit on two pages?

How complex is the story? Will we need to provide any further backup, such as a fact sheet, bios, and additional artwork?

Does the boilerplate information about the firm in the release match the message/expertise being showcased?

Will a reporter or reader who visits our Web site for further information find complementary or conflicting messages and information?

In what other forms can we use this release to maximize its effectiveness?

If all the answers add up to "go!" you'll surely also find ways to use the story in a variety of marketing situations. But if the answers add up to "uh-oh!" you'll save yourself time and money, and your firm from being embarrassed, by holding off on releasing the story. Do this twenty-question drill, and you'll know what can be done when the time is right.

The purpose of this exercise is not to throw cold water on your enthusiasm. Rather, it's to tune-up the effort, inspire you to use your resources effectively, and make sure that—whatever you communicate—you'll get the most benefit in return.

You may have noticed that the same kinds of questions pertain to marketing, period, and to public relations, period. In short, get your strategic ducks in a row; the rest will fall easily into place.

PRINCIPLE 22

Don't start anything you can't finish

The best way to learn is from your own mistakes. The second best way—surely less painful—is to learn from the mistakes of others. Here are four case studies of top-flight firms who let the parade pass them by. Read 'em and weep.

Case Study 1: We had gained the confidence of an excellent civil engineering firm in New England that had created a very valuable piece of real estate by bridging over the main turnpike into a major city. Wanting to be known for this project and specialized work, the firm hired us to create a basic information package about its air-rights design, a new concept at the time. Our then-young office had to produce a variety of storylines that would appeal to a range of readers, as well as generate visuals, bios of the key people, and whatever information would be needed to attract the media read by these engineers' client and consultant base. The engineering firm figured its constituency was state or city DOTs, developers, architects, land-use planners, community groups, and the like.

We reasoned that placing one good article in the best publication read by each of these constituent groups would be the right strategy, and we were able to achieve this goal. We also added a leading consulting engineering publication for purposes of professional advancement and recruitment. As the response to these pieces started to roll in, we announced to our client that we were now ready to develop the reprints, cover letters, and mailings that would take these materials right to the desks of the people these civil engineers wanted to reach.

But after all our efforts—the necessary photography, presentation drawings, and other expenses—it turned out that the principal in charge of business development didn't have additional budget for the payload phase. He never planned for it. His goal: Reach the one person who would hire his firm after having read the article. Our goal: Get the information moving and keep turning it over in an efficient, effective sequence, so our client's name would be on everyone's mind and lips. It never dawned on us—recently-minted consultants working with clients new to public relations—to ask whether he had allocated sufficient funds to see the project through.

Regardless of what people say, what they really want to achieve is to get more work. Put the available budget at the top of the agenda at the public relations campaign planning meeting. If the budget can't support a full-court press, what can it permit? Over how long a period? What results does the firm want, and what are those results worth?

Case Study 2: Even if a marketing staff includes someone trained in public relations, much of that person's time is taken up in the day-to-day writing and activities of a busy office. Because I've been there, done that, I know how RFPs that materialize two days before they are due have a way of absorbing and exhausting the marketing team.

In this case, a national architecture and planning firm with multiple offices and a competent marketing staff hired us to get the firm's name known for its regional approach to design management. We were making great headway, forging language, getting articles placed, and arranging speaking opportunities.

The marketing troops were responsive when we needed background, even though they were not remotely interested in working with the media.

Nonetheless, the firm's nonmarketing principals wondered why they had so many people on the marketing staff and still this campaign was being done outside. Their goal was to save money by making better use of the home team.

But the marketing principal for whom we worked had different goals: Reposition the firm and get more work in new sectors. Missing from the list, however, was: Build consensus among the partners for the plan to reposition the firm. The marketing principal was thus unable to persuade the other principals to continue retaining an outside firm or to overcome their frugality. Halfway through a two-year campaign, we turned the project over to the marketing department. It was one of the few times I've actually raised my voice to a client, imploring him not to do something ("undo" is a more apt word choice). And, yes, the project stopped cold. All that investment was wasted.

Case Study 3: A West Coast firm of planners and architects had been given an exceptional commission to replicate a U.S. resort region in Asia. The firm stressed how important this would be in a hard-driving country that was just learning the importance of leisure activities. What an assignment for them! What a storyline for us to work with!

They instructed us to inform similar companies in the U.S. and the Pacific Rim of the commission and about the skilled planners available to do this kind of project. We even gained permission from the Asian client to proceed, no small achievement.

Everything was in order. We gave the design firm a mock-up of our press kit—release, visuals (architectural renderings, a map), fact sheet on the project, description of the people behind the project, a profile of the firm—and they pronounced it . . . visually dull. Forget the fact that the materials were well written and their format was the accepted norm worldwide.

Our goal: Get the story out. Their goal: Make a lovely package. With only a two-week window of opportunity, reluctantly we surrendered the kit to our client for redesign. One month went by, two months . . . the firm got busy doing that project and others, and the materials never went out.

Case Study 4: I've learned stoicism where the press is concerned. Editors leave or publications fold while you're in the middle of developing the story-of-a-lifetime. My version of Murphy's Law pertains: The more crucial it is to you, the larger the obstacles in your path.

We have always treated editors respectfully, which they genuinely appreciate. Their lives, like most of the people in the building industry, are run by immutable deadlines. Our goal: Make both our client *and* the editor shine.

We had gotten our client a major placement: a bylined essay in a prominent design magazine—in its annual big issue, no less. We expected to help with the shaping, writing, fact-checking, and illustrating of the article. No, said the client, proudly; I'll take it from here. Though following up is our mode, we backed off.

His goal? That's the point of this case study. The editor called three days after the absolute final deadline to say that he hadn't heard from the author, had we? Our fellow had become involved in a number of essential projects and ignored the fact

that the deadline was upon him. Miracles happen; he immediately hunkered down and submitted an acceptable manuscript.
But in the scheme of things, the author and everyone in his
firm will be lucky if the magazine decides to rely on them in
the future.

What's to be learned from these four sad tales of wasted time
and money? Performance is judged at the finish line.

PRINCIPLE 23

Divide people into three categories

Curiously, trios are helpful when seeking to understand and evaluate a firm's dynamic.

For instance, years ago I came across this adage in a business magazine: "There are three kinds of people in any organization—finders, minders, and grinders."

In the case of a design industry business, the finders are often the founding generation of owners: they have to find clients, offices, consultants, cash, and staff.

Minders are the finders' right-hand people, without whom there would be no firm. In some architecture offices, I've heard minders referred to as "pencils," meaning that Bill, the minder, draws up what Bob, the finder, wants designed. Bob, as a finder, can then refine what he doesn't have the time to develop himself. These valuable minders serve as the finders' second set of eyes and ears, and they know the finders' wishes better than anyone.

Minders are found in the inner circle of leadership because they often carry the major client work. Rarely, however, are they responsible for finding clients or for building the firm's good name—although they are usually deeply involved in maintaining client relationships. Making a finder corps out of minders can be a challenging public relations assignment.

Some minders exist entirely in the shadow of the One Great Man who is the real reason for the firm's existence. One such practice asked us to audit its client base when its eminent star died, leaving others in the firm, at long last, in control. The survivors wanted to know what people thought of *them* as an office. While I am in favor of benchmark research, this assignment came from their concern that there might not be a future without their leader, rather than from their desire to learn what they needed to adapt from their past in order to make their future happen. The firm, though a group of superlative professionals, struggled and then vanished.

Grinders could be considered the tribe in the drafting room or back office—those who really grind out the work. Yet, the next generation of finders may come from that firm's restless grinders. Look for this talent and develop it, even if it means running the risk that a well-trained younger professional will leave the firm to start another one.

A while back, then-thirty-two-year-old Ted Hammer stopped by my office at HLW, where I was director of communications. With a most serious mien, he asked me what it would take for him to become a partner. Because he was so terribly earnest, and after I recovered from the shock that this upstart actually imagined himself running such a venerable place, we laid out his strategy. What a movie that transformation would make! A year later, having made all the other right moves and consequently having brought in a prodigious project, Ted became HLW's youngest partner ever.

When I have a chance to meet with a project team in the course of being briefed about that office's work, I'll sometimes see a "Ted," trying hard to move himself and the firm ahead. When I ask the principals to keep an eye out for that person and help with his or her career development, often they'll be ing the grinders for their potential.

"Management, marketing, public relations—not one of them can afford people who watch and wonder. Sometimes principals even stop things from happening. For instance, they don't participate in the development and evolution of the firm's marketing and public relations plans and budget. They don't support or monitor the work of the marketing group. They deny their marketers the time, equipment, or information requested. They stall on paying fees to photographers and graphic designers.

So business development opportunities falter or don't happen. It's only a matter of time before there is grumbling in principals' meetings about the attitude of the overburdened marketing people. But where *do* the problems start?

The final threesome came to me from Roz Burak, a management coach who consults to design firms and with whom we have worked as well. Roz says there are three kinds of people: "Starters, doers, and completers."

I took exception when she described me as a "completer." Didn't I spend my days starting things for our clients, creating concepts and events that never existed before, and making things happen? "Okay," Roz conceded, "but you also see them through. A lot of creative people start things and then never set the strategy for their completion. That's disappointing and wasteful. Plus, in a firm, that behavior can also be exhausting and demoralizing."

You have to be there; you can't phone it in

This has not been a good century so far for corporate leaders—or, for that matter, religious, nonprofit, and academic leaders. When the federal government gets involved, you know that the problem is out of hand. It's remarkable that Americans, increasingly cynical about leadership, still recognize the importance of having excellent, in fact exceptional, people at the helm of an organization.

At the same time that leadership is understandably under such enormous scrutiny, public relations research recently revealed that a CEO's reputation can represent nearly fifty percent of a company's reputation. Half! That will tell you how crucial it is for leaders to be able to communicate well.

Does the same math hold true for leaders in the professional services sector? Even more so. After all, in the world of commerce, leaders come and go, but leaders in the design and construction realm—especially when they are the founding principals—feel that they are there for life.

Federal Reserve Chairman Alan Greenspan has weighed in on the matter. At the 1999 Harvard commencement, he addressed the value of a good reputation: "In today's world, where ideas are increasingly displacing the physical in the production of economic value, competition for reputation becomes a significant driving force, propelling our country forward. Manufactured goods often can be evaluated before the completion of their transaction. Service providers, on the other hand, can offer only their reputations."

Most of the time, employees and even partners don't grasp the importance of the titular head of the firm. That fifty percent statistic offers a powerful motivation to evaluate how effectively the CEO sets and verbalizes the firm's agenda, inspires staff to perform at the highest level, articulates purpose and consensus in a merger, persuades great clients to join the roster, negotiates coherently for the firm, convinces a journalist to cover or ignore something that happened, lucidly represents the firm in all kinds of outside forums, and voices strength in times of stress. Obviously, it is essential for the CEO to think with clarity and then communicate equally clearly in all these situations.

Can leaders be turned into good communicators? Not everyone wants to be; not everyone can be. I've coached and advised a long list of leaders in this community. People who start firms or take them over may be good businesspeople, visionaries, or mavericks, but not necessarily natural communicators. They may also be shy or lack taste, an accurate if old-fashioned word. And while it's tough enough to run a firm, especially one composed of creative people, even CEOs who are up for that challenge might flinch at the thought of addressing a gathering of principals or staff, speaking publicly, or being interviewed by a reporter.

The size of the firm or the nature of the business doesn't matter. The leader has to make a point, support it with a good story, and get the principles involved heard, understood, and acted upon.

One freshly arrived construction-company CEO had at his disposal economic projections galore for the company, the industry, and the client base. However, it quickly became 141 apparent that he had come to his new post with no anecdotes to share, not even a book on his night table that he could quote. An experienced and effective businessman, obviously with a generous salary and stature, still he hadn't worked on those skills. Instead, he remained an uncomfortable communicator who underarticulated his points. Sometimes people who reach this level of authority don't reach for help—in fact, may not even realize how much they need it, until they face public-speaking occasions. In this case, his inability to speak compellingly so concerned the members of his staff that they tactfully arranged for outside assistance.

On the other side of the coin is the legendary Bill Caudill. During his long career, the 1984 AIA Gold Medalist and founder of CRS wrote some 4,000 statements, his "TIBs," many of which he compiled in a book titled *This I Believe*. The book is long out of print, but you can get a weekly dose of this superb communicator's observations by subscribing to an archive at Texas A&M University.

In the book's introduction, Thomas A. Bullock, then chairman of the CRS board, tackled the question of why Caudill wrote them. Here's Caudill's own answer, as quoted by Bullock: "'To pinpoint things we really believe in? To encourage and express the openness that characterizes our company? To communicate thoughts on current issues? To produce responses? To carry on a continual writing of our history? Paper therapy? Perhaps all of these.'"

Bullock continues: "Probably the best answer is that Bill wanted to improve his thinking by expressing himself regularly in clear, simple thoughts." He goes on to quote Caudill again: "'Most of us need to write and think.'"

The third example of communication at the top comes from one of my first consulting jobs. Our client, an engineer at the helm of an architecture firm begun by his father, had a salty vocabulary and unequaled bravado. The practice was being assailed because a large public project had gone awry, not really his firm's fault, as an investigation later discovered. But the newspapers loved the scandal; one of them regularly used its front page to howl its displeasure. This is not the way to be on Page One.

Most firm leaders—though, as will be apparent, not this one—know that what they say publicly can be misinterpreted, so they are careful. Early one Saturday morning in the middle of the fracas, the reporter tracking the saga called and caught our hero still in bed. "Engineer Claims State Is Stirring the Bloody Soup," was the breathtaking banner headline the next morning in the state's most important daily, in its largest-circulation issue.

Clearly this was not going well, and with headlines like that, just as clearly the story would go on forever, shaking both his clients' and staff's faith in the firm. I gingerly inquired why he had given the reporter that sensational quote. "I didn't!" he responded indignantly. What he actually told the reporter is not appropriate to repeat here, any more than in that article, let it be said. I said a quiet prayer of thanks that the reporter hadn't fired with all barrels and convinced our loudmouth to transfer the task of dealing with the press to a more measured partner.

Given that fifty percent of an organization's reputation rests with its CEO, along with evidence gleaned from these anecdotes, it's obvious how important it is for any organization's titular leader to submit to a good reality check about how he or she speaks, writes, appears, and socializes. Actually, the entire leadership should be assessed—by itself as a group, by the marketing department, or by a tactful outside consultant. Then it's easy enough to get coaching in these skills, whether privately outside the office or internally one-on-one or as a group.

Nowadays, some firms won't even consider hiring someone for a senior position who doesn't have excellent communication skills. And lest you think that engineers, often faulted for their lack of communication skills, are off the hook, you should know that Cooper Union now offers a public-speaking course in its liberal arts curriculum to train its engineering students.

Warren Bennis, founding chairman of the University of Southern California's Leadership Institute, was once interviewed for a behavioral sciences Web site about how people prepare to become leaders. Among other things, he advised the following: "Provide terrific role models because, as we all know, modeling is one of the best ways to 'teach' leadership. That goes for good and bad role models. Often, we learn the most from negative role models."

What you resist, persists

The catchphrase "What you resist, persists" is not a law of physics; to the extent of my research, it is a New Age maxim. I've observed in my own office and in our consulting work that the more time people spend complaining about something, the less time, energy, and inclination they have to deal with the situation. Their resistance to improving the situation permits their problem to fester.

Absorbed by their resistance, these people can't see their options clearly. How *can* anyone move in a positive direction when they are sidetracked, frustrated, annoyed, worried, vexed, disturbed, embarrassed—any of the hundred other adjectives that describe a state of anger?

After filling all the other pages of this book with things to consider and do, the resist/persist principle inspires a "*not* to do" list. Two items head this restraining list: The first is working with clients who don't want you to make a profit. The second is thinking that a problematic employee—or partner—will magically become an ideal one. Cut it out!

Do not work with clients who don't want you to make a profit.

A few years ago, Dick Ostop of Newfield Construction in Connecticut weighed in on the topic of what constitutes a good or a bad client. I had set up a conference program on client management and retention. During his cameo appearance, Dick explained his philosophy: "Clients who represent legitimate growth opportunities are a worthy investment of your resources, beyond those necessary to provide excellent service. And, a lot of firms don't like changing architects, engineers, and contractors; instead, they pick a group and work with them. Some, though, go to the bottom of the market: low bid, best price. Do you want *that* for a client? I don't."

Preparing for the conference, my office had polled design and construction firms around the country to learn how their offices handle an unfortunate selection of client or deal with a client's unfortunate choice of project or program manager. We asked these firms, "Do you have the will and a way to move aside clients without offending them?" "At what point do you talk to the client about the issues?" And, "You give your client the right to oblige you to change *your* project manager; can you ask for a change if his project representative gets in the way of progress?"

The survey results surprised me, including one blunt retort: "Deal with it. The client is always right." Always? What vows did that respondent take upon becoming a professional?

If a client proves to be so difficult, you must already have uncovered some concerns during the business development phase of the relationship. If you can't achieve open communication with the client from the start of the project, if each member of the team and the client can't clearly state what they want jointly and individually from the project, and if the differences in style once the job is underway lead to disarray rather than admiration, then you simply can't do that job to your best professional standards.

Refusing an opportunity before or in the middle of the work is a serious decision; of course, there will be consequences. Still, counseled Leonardo da Vinci, perhaps referring to his working relationship with one of his Renaissance patrons, "It's easier to resist at the beginning than at the end."

As soon as the issue surfaces, you might ask yourself, "Whom would we harm by continuing on this path?" Not coincidentally, that question is part of the litmus test for a discussion of ethics. Using the question to examine an uncomfortable client relationship puts your discomfort in perspective: What *are* your professional obligations? To whom are they owed?

Back to the results of our survey about how different firms handle difficult clients: One design office said it changes people internally to make the relationship work; in fact, the firm won't assign a project leader until it is clear whom the client has appointed as its representative. Another firm stares the compatibility problem square in the face, seeking to be sure that its own people haven't been the source of the situation: "We have instituted a strong *relationship*-quality program in our firm, and charged the committee with identifying possible areas of conflict with clients along with suggesting ways to avoid or resolve them. This is a tremendous check and balance within the project team." A third office just toughs out the relationship: "We give the project manager combat pay for putting up with a difficult client." (I am not sure what that approach accomplishes.)

"Find clients who value what you can do for them," advises author Jim Camp in *Start with No*, a contrarian book on negotiating. Kate Keating, an environmental graphic designer, tells a story about saying no to a vexing client relationship. Kate's San Francisco–based firm had triumphed in an extensive selection process. "We were elated to have won that very big job. Then the fun part started: negotiations," Kate relates. "We sat down and talked scope, went back, and wrote a fee proposal—

and the client was floored at the cost. They had budgeted total-ly inadequately."

"What design firm hasn't had this experience?" Kate won-ders, philosophically. "I knew we couldn't do this job in the manner in which we work, without compromising the project and demoralizing our people. So we stepped aside. But we part-ed as friends, which helped keep our reputation intact."

It takes fortitude to resign from a job, especially one that promises prestige and has been so hard-won. But Kate made every effort to handle the situation well. She was selected because the client believed her firm would be able to make the right choices and control its aspect of the project; in deciding to walk away, she demonstrated her ability to make prudent choices—for both her practice *and* the client.

Another excellent graphic designer, Roger Whitehouse of Whitehouse & Company in New York, with whom we often work, declares that, "Facing facts, we have an allegiance to our profession and its values, and to the project as well. That some-times comes before our allegiance to our client—although the client is a very close second."

I've coached principals through we-can't-continue-like-this moments in their client relationships. We discuss how to tact-fully but not necessarily subtly communicate their perception and grievance to their client in a way that also permits all par-ties to listen and resolve the problem.

After all these preparations, after the difficult discussion is over, the best outcome is not the handshake with the client. Rather, it's the reaction of those in the office and, in particular, the team, reinvigorated because its work has been supported.

2. Do *not* put up with a problematic employee.

Dale Carnegie observed that "any fool can criticize, condemn, and complain, and most do." Does that describe someone who reports to you?

What is the purpose of holding on to an employee who is not the right fit? Certainly, employers look for people who will further the firm's goals. We have even written job descriptions for our clients that include—besides the specifics of the work and level of technological literacy—the mission for the firm, a description of its culture, the reason for the position, and the qualities that are the starting point for consideration for the job.

Firms that want such precise and complete job descriptions certainly must use them to guide candidate interviews and reference checks. Their ability to frankly discuss their expectations signals their commitment to open communication with their employees.

An employee who does something horrific will, of course, be dismissed instantly. One who undermines the client relationship will ultimately, though regrettably, spark a firestorm with that client. But what about something less obvious—for example, people who don't sustain the firm's culture? One office hired a young professional whose bright personality was a plus for the position. What no one spotted was that her previous employer expected her to take a project off his hands, produce it on her own, and then bring it back. As it turned out, she preferred to work in isolation and, therefore, had no way to fit in the collaborative culture of the office. No amount of mentoring, outside courses, or reviews could change such a fundamental difference. She was released.

In the early days of my business, I scratched together enough funds to ask a well-known management consultant to public relations firms to assess whether we had gotten off on the right foot. Among other things, he told me to fire someone every six months, an action that would foster a nose-to-the-grindstone attitude with all the other employees. Anyone in particular, I asked anxiously, since I didn't have many employees at that point and tend to get attached to good people? Without a likely candidate, he responded, the choice would be totally mine. That advice still perplexes me—I don't follow it—but when I mention it to other business owners, it always gets a knowing smile. Triage? Hmmmm.

Many people hope that the situation with an employee who doesn't measure up, causes dissension, ignores the rules, and consistently disappoints or antagonizes clients will somehow right itself. There's an old joke that goes, "One day as I sat sad and dreary, a voice came to me out of the gloom saying, 'Cheer up! Things could be worse.' So I cheered up, and sure enough, things got worse."

In an interview in *Fast Company*, turnaround consultant (and former Chilean minister of finance) Fernando Flores comments sternly, "Hope is the raw material of losers." What happens when troublesome people remain in the firm, even after warnings and attempts to modify the behavior? They conclude that they are welcome to continue creating havoc. Even worse, other staff members lose faith not only in that person but also in the principals.

More than once, I've been asked to help with damage control when a self-righteous employee who overstayed but was then fired went to former clients and the media with detrimental and dramatic insider tales. Whether or not the tales are true, it's hard to admit at that point that the leadership didn't see this situation coming, and harder yet to accept that staff members may have spotted (and endured) problems but chosen not to address them with the principals. To what or whom were *they* being loyal?

There may even come a point at which principals and partners—the post, not the title, is relevant—need to be released from their responsibilities. Performance can skid, or people may have been elevated beyond their willingness to shoulder responsibility and to grow. Because of their highly visible position within the office, their breakdown will be fairly obvious to everyone, starting at the front desk. For that alone, resistance to dealing with the predicament is not an option for the other leaders of the firm.

A problem of this magnitude demands very precise, very direct communication and action from the leadership group. Un-partner, reassign, or release: Your credibility is on the line.

At the least, try for goodwill at any separation, if it is possible and merited. Word gets around. Be clear within your office and with the departing person—you both should sign a written agreement—precisely what story you will be telling the world.

What's to be learned from such experiences? In *The Journal of Negative Results*, a new peer-reviewed biomedical journal, some scientists have tried to formalize an approach by providing scientists and physicians "with responsible and balanced information in order to improve experimental designs and clinical decisions." The journal's founders were frustrated that all they ever read or heard about were the positive results of research, which leaves the rest of the community in the dark about what didn't work. They call this "negative data." Worse yet, they feel that such a void condemns researchers to repeat trials unnecessarily. With people's health and lives in the balance, they reason, anything that can increase research speed is essential.

Except for the storyline of *The Producers*, no one sets out intentionally to fail. Accumulating negative results is just part of life in any business. What most firms don't do, however, is contemplate their negative data. Incidentally, Ben Franklin didn't like that word "fail." "I haven't failed," he said, "I've found 10,000 ways that don't work."

It doesn't matter that you find the situation a nuisance, that it creates stress, or that you fervently wish you were not the person who must deal with it. The important thing is to assess what happened and why, who was harmed, and how the sequence of events could be remedied for all time.

Coming face to face with what you value—and have temporarily lost—will inspire you to formulate powerful principles that will guide your future commitments. (How specifically to do this is the message and method of the last chapter.)

PRINCIPLE 26

Get connected

Imagine this recruitment advertisement: Do you want to be sought after and known as influential? Informed? Able to have politicians and community leaders return your phone call? Visionary? Communicative? Effective? Admired?

The sponsor of that ad could be any one of the dozens of associations that support the design and building industry, locally, regionally, or nationally. But this recruitment is not optional. In addition to being personally and professionally responsible, you must also be actively engaged.

People become involved in association work for many reasons. Besides the obvious obligations, the mandatory education credits, and certain prerogatives, associations provide an outlet for fulfillment that many professionals don't find in their firms: a rapid path to leadership, access to authoritative community organizers, and the chance to meet like-minded people.

Peter Drucker is forceful on the topic of nonprofit organizations. His *Managing the Non-Profit Organization*, now out of print but worth finding, includes these lines: "[A nonprofit organization's] mission and leadership are not just things to read about, to listen to. They are things to do something about. Things that you can, and should, convert from good intentions and from knowledge into effective action, not next year, but tomorrow morning."

When professionals say they don't have time to participate in the meetings, events, advocacy, or projects sponsored by their associations—or protest that the organizations are not worth investing in—they are forgetting the important contributions of their organizations. Among these contributions are establishing and codifying standards, creating a body of knowledge, fighting injustice or imbalance, bringing like-minded folk together for a common purpose, recording the history of the community, and keeping its future alive and meaningful.

People also forget the usefulness of being involved in association work. Associations enable their members to sharpen their skills in speaking, developing events, and management. The first balance sheet I had to master was when I was the treasurer of an organization. Involvement in associations also bumps up the members' marketing and recruitment opportunities.

Here are some ways in which associations serve their constituents' goals and objectives, and how your firm can benefit from being involved:

To advance an issue or rectify a grievance, form or join a group to research the larger situation and formulate a course of action. Invite the key players to address a small or public forum on the issue. Officials will come to a meeting that has been organized by a reputable organization, whereas they might not give you time privately. In fact, get several associations involved and arrange a cross-disciplinary program. More people will attend, your contact list will grow, and—not to ignore the primary objective—your issue and its possible resolution will come into focus.

To become a force in the community, assume leadership—of either a committee or the entire organization. Endless meetings and obligations? Of course, that's part of it; you have taken on a demanding second job. But you become the industry's spokesperson. Is there any place you can't go with that credential?

To protest counterproductive legislation or agency rules and procedures, create the organization's task force specifically charged with informing and getting feedback from the community, as well as the targeted agencies and politicians. Articulate the position of the association membership, and draft its official statement. Write and circulate an op-ed piece; in fact, work with the local media to enlighten citizens and create support. Negotiate the language that will be substituted for the offending regulations.

To get the bigger picture, join peer task forces or councils. Many industry organizations set up programs to attract younger members. By so doing, they ignore their senior professionals, and then wonder why they don't come to meetings.

Many organizations offer such opportunities. The Urban Land Institute does it particularly well. ULI sets up weeklong development-related project teams that provide invaluable advice to local communities. What's in it for the team members, who work intensively without compensation? They get out of the office and their own comfort zone of authority, enjoy a different kind of challenge, draw on all their skills where the greater good is the impetus, and forge working relationships among themselves that have value long after the analysis is over.

There are some caveats, of course. For instance, associations have the same constraints as any enterprise: Don't run at a loss, keep the "customers" satisfied, and maintain good records. If they are not managed well, however, that's as much the fault of the constituents as the staff. Sometimes the last people to understand how this works are the volunteers.

Occasionally, associations adopt an unfortunate us/them attitude. Staff complaints about thoughtless members are valid.
Whatever your level of engagement, it pays to treat association
staff as courteously as valued colleagues. If there is no staff liai-
son to your committee, get one assigned, so there is even less
chance for friction. Know your limits and be clear with the staff
as well as with your committee members what you can and can't
do, and won't be able to do. Learn what they can afford to do,
given their resources, and adjust accordingly. Communicate to
the executive director if things are not going well, agree on the
standard of performance, and see what can be done to improve
the level of service.

Volunteers truly deserve special handling. They are not doing
association work for the paycheck; they have another tab running. When you recruit members for a specific assignment, it
helps to hear from them what they expect to achieve over the
year for the organization, the profession, and themselves.
Perhaps I should put this in boldface: When you articulate your
own and your committee's agenda within the association's
agenda, also find out what everyone who reports to you on the
committee plans to achieve during the year, and how.

It never fails to surprise me how many people initially get
involved in committee work "because I was asked" but then
remain clueless and ineffective. You have just given them a
chance to help the profession, community, society—and themselves; they need a wake-up call!

In *How Firms Succeed: A Field Guide to Design Management*,
co-authors James P. Cramer of Greenway Consulting and Scott
Simpson of The Stubbins Group comment on authority: "In a
very real sense, authority is like an electrical circuit—it carries

no current unless it is connected at both ends. . . . The trick is to get people to respond properly."

Your volunteer members also deserve visibility, including gracious thanks. This is the one place to always use "we" abundantly and to communicate that the group is responsible for the success of the activities, even if it's been tough going.

As for assignments, your committee or board vice-chairman isn't appointed to wait out the year until he takes the helm; his intangible role is to maintain continuity, so initiatives undertaken in past and current years flourish under his leadership. Your treasurer isn't there to ensure that the accounting firm gets the figures in on time for the annual meeting; her role is to ensure that the organization is solvent enough to move ahead with major as well as routine projects. Your membership chairman isn't appointed just to plump up the roster and bring in new revenue through the new dues; his real, and risky, role is to identify the next generation of leaders.

Some people put association work on their résumés and then walk away. They even note the specific committees to which they have added their names. This makes me cranky. If I have volunteered our committee to take on a responsibility, but certain members don't support these activities—in fact, don't even show up—I don't ignore them; I ask them to resign.

One bit of housekeeping: For all the years that I have been involved with associations in various capacities, I find that the committee-level record keeping is negligible. One of my favorite organizations can't even find its bylaws! Without a resident memory or records, just how effective can an association be as it passes from one regime to the next? What does happen to all those reports, announcements, press releases, and contact lists that should go in the archives? Why do they vanish like children's socks at camp? How, for instance, can you serve effectively on a nominating committee without an accurate record of what posts people have previously held?

You can also bring the association to your location. I have been in offices where the design or construction firm's meeting rooms and lobbies are used routinely by the local Chamber of Commerce, nonprofit boards, and industry associations. Some firms—most notably those that specialize in hospitality and a number of law offices—carve out and fit up a "conference center." One lighting designer/manufacturer that moved into a well-located, renovated factory made available a well-illuminated (by definition), generously sized portion of the space for local associations to meet at no charge. Smart thinking.

Providing meeting space costs little more than an urn of coffee, ice, and some sodas, but it creates exceptional goodwill and traffic. Don't turn these events over entirely to the marketing or administrative staff. Hang around to greet the group; one of the attendees might be someone you've been trying to reach for months.

Another way to bring the association into the firm also amortizes the potentially high cost of association membership and involvement. Every staff member whose dues are paid by the firm, including the principals, should be active in the association and should also share with the rest of the office any information learned, materials gathered, and connections made. This could be in a memo, an article in the in-house newsletter, and/or a presentation. This accountability encourages meaningful engagement, good listening habits, and note-taking skills; repeating content yields experience in training others. If your designated association member leaves the firm, arrange to have the membership transferred to someone else, when possible.

Here's a situation where, by using an association connection, we were able to transform an architect with ambitions, but no connections, in historic preservation into a member of the inner circle. At our urging, our client had joined the Historic Preservation Committee of the New York chapter of the AIA. We thought he'd take a while to get acclimated; instead, he immediately volunteered to do an event.

If you're going to do an event, might as well make it major, I always say. It was, we pointed out to him, the eve of the 30th anniversary of the Landmarks Preservation legislation in New York City. We suggested that he propose to his committee a panel discussion on whether the legislation still had validity, since there appeared to be only street clocks and trees left to designate.

Three months later, a sellout crowd of 150 sat and stood through a program that fielded the Landmarks Commissioner; the house counsel for the commission; the late Brendan Gill of *The New Yorker*, a ranking preservationist and great citizen of New York; and our architect.

Here's what it took to muster and also to attract that audience. My office stage-managed the entire event, although I doubt that the committee even knew. Working occasionally with committee members and AIA staff, our client and his office

Invited the panel by letter, phone, and follow-up call.

Set up the announcement and promotion to chapter members, and turned it over to chapter staff to handle, including reservations.

Met individually with each panel member to brief him or her on appropriate timing and content.

Hosted a teleconference to coordinate the presentations.

Secured the location and arranged for a small, related display.

Considered the cost of a modest reception and set a price to attend.

Compiled a list and invited VIPs from other city watchdog organizations, notably those with preservation responsibilities, in his name as committee chair.

Alerted officers of AIA New York about the significance of the milestone and thus the event, invited the chapter president to be the convener, and provided the introductory text.

Invited select members of the general, design, and preservation press to attend.

Researched and wrote a brief illustrated history of the Landmarks law in practice to be delivered at the start of the event (one challenge: our client was terrified of speaking in public).

Obtained the official bios of the speakers and developed them into a single narrative sheet that was handed to attendees.

Organized the check-in desk; appointed a committee member to be the greeter at the door and briefed him.

Appointed another committee member to be responsible for specific requests from the speakers at the event itself.

Called the day before to be sure that everything and everyone was set.

Figured out the best seating configuration, and then supervised the setting up of the room.

Taped the event to have a record for the committee and also to answer any later press inquiries.

Hosted a dinner afterward at a nearby restaurant to thank the panel (and, of course, included the partners of the firm).

Wrote the panelists to thank them for their time and the exceptional results.

Wrote and distributed a press release in the next few days, along with photos from the event.

Provided this release to a limited list of clients and prospective clients, as well.

Seems like a lot of effort? Agreed. Was it worth it? In three months, starting from relative obscurity, there wasn't a person in the preservation community who didn't know this architect's name and firm name. He had learned the governing legislation and pertinent case studies. He had earned the respect of the audience and the chapter leadership. He even realized that he could speak in public without passing out (although there was a moment when we thought the size of the audience had overwhelmed him). More to the point, within a few months the firm had preservation projects under way.

All of this proves the exhortation by David Lloyd George, England's prime minister at the height of World War I: "Don't be afraid to take a big step, if one is indicated. You can't cross a chasm in two small jumps."

PRINCIPLE 27

Listen generously

In the early 1990s the American Institute of Architects commissioned the Roper Organization to research how clients select architects. Roper's response was enlightening: Clients look first for professionals who listen and respond well to their needs and goals. (No. 2 was the ability to deal with public agencies. "Money" was much farther down the list.)

Listening is the basis of trust and negotiation, and the lack of listening is cited as one of the reasons mergers fail. It's wise to remember a celebrated passage from Ecclesiastes: There is "a time to keep silence, and a time to speak."

Given the obvious importance of listening, why do some people tune out and let their mind wander? Or argue, fake attention, and react strongly to emotional words? Or consider the subject uninteresting and concentrate instead on the speaker's delivery? Or interrupt the speaker, finish his or her thoughts, avoid eye contact, and change the topic? Or anticipate what's going to be said and formulate a response even before the other person has finished speaking?

Research indicates that the average listener hears, understands, evaluates properly, and retains only about half of what was said during a brief presentation within a few hours. And within 48 hours, retention drops to a quarter. If you find this hard to believe, ask your consultants or staff members to repeat the instructions you have just given them. See how close they come.

We are very skilled at half-listening to people when they are speaking. Think of how often you are doing something else while listening to the radio or the television, or someone on your cell phone.

Early in my experience as a consultant, when my listening skills were not yet quite in place, we had gotten a firm of mechanical/electrical/plumbing consulting engineers as a new client. I was impatient to get to work and dismayed that week after week, all we seemed to do was meet with all seven partners. There was no marketing plan and certainly no business plan from which to start, so we gamely inquired about how they operated and what was important to them.

These sessions would start at 5:30, after their client work was put aside. The office manager would unlock the cabinet in the conference room where she kept the Milano cookies, and these principals—all but the lead partner legendarily nonverbal—would amazingly talk on (and on) until their commuter trains were on post-rush hour schedules.

We had been hired to create a new approach, new vocabulary, and new materials, but we seemed to be adrift. Finally, convinced that it was a better idea to resign the account than be fired for nonperformance, I invited the partner in charge of marketing to join me for breakfast. Clearly, it was a mismatch, I told him, regretfully; everything seemed to have stalled.

He was genuinely stunned at my declaration, and I was in turn surprised by his response: "This is the first time in the history of the practice that all the partners have come into one room at one time to discuss the future of the firm. We really appreciate how you are bringing us into focus."

So, what I thought was a failure was actually, to these engineers, the best-ever start of something truly important. I just hadn't focused on—you might say "heard"—what was really happening. Moreover, since this was the first time an outside communications consultant had worked with their firm, they were a lot more excited by the process than they let on. I was very lucky that I swallowed my pride and spoke up. Everybody had a good laugh. The work that resulted was very useful, and the collaboration all by itself was a source of pride.

Listen generously. Listen with an open mind for what's really being said, and for what isn't said. Mozart believed that "the silences between the notes are as important as the notes themselves." Ask a question and listen to learn whether the question you asked is really being answered—and if it's some other question that is being answered, why is that? What's more important to the conversation: the answer you sought or what the speaker is saying? Do the speaker's words have purpose, so they can be acted on? What is the speaker's central theme?

Ears aren't the only listening mechanism you possess. Your eyes also notice "body language," which is harder to control than language. Mannerisms are particularly revealing. For that reason, if we have to conduct a particularly sensitive interview of a client or a client's conduct, we prefer to do it face to face.

Jean-Pierre LaCroix, an environmental graphic designer from Toronto, works from the principle of "listen and you will be heard." Known for being very persuasive, J.P. says that listening is "all about clearly understanding the client's needs and being sympathetic to what he's asking you to do. That entails both understanding the challenges that the client faces—

beyond what he thinks is the problem—and getting to know his business."

Q: Well then, J.P., how do you convince your client that what he's asked for is wrong, particularly if he's already defined the solution in his mind?

A: "You have to present back to him his perceived solution, to show how well you listened. Then, you show him the big picture and how the original solution limits opportunities. Finally, once you've convinced him that you care about his business, that it's not just another assignment, you can present your solution."

Many years ago, a senior public relations professional gave me some tips on how to listen. "Your client only wants to look good," he explained. "Ask questions. Let him talk himself out. Say to him, 'That's quite a story.' Otherwise, don't even respond. When he says there's a problem, don't say that you've dealt with it before. Find out what he's really thinking about, what he wants from you. Ask him to develop his thought a little more fully. Save anything you have to say until the end. He'll be convinced you're the smartest consultant he's ever known."

People listen from their own perspective. All the filters were in place when I recently led a client's marketing-team meeting. I asked that the people around the table share their notes with me, since I was certain I would be too engaged in the dynamics of the meeting to make a reliable record for myself

What I observed—when four very different sets of minutes came to me, with one person abstaining—was that each of them was in the room, alert and engaged, but each had attended a different meeting. As TV personality Diane Sawyer comments,

"The one lesson I have learned is that there is no substitute for paying attention."

PRINCIPLE 28

Let go

Many professionals—and I admit I am one of them—work long hours to be sure the work is done right and delivered on time. "Want to have two careers?" goes the old taunt: "Work 80 hours a week!" Many practitioners put in these long hours uncomplainingly. They love what they do and feel that they have just so much time available to them to improve the planet by applying their talent and skills.

Ironically, part of the appeal of becoming a principal is the freedom to control your own time, as well as call the shots. There's a conundrum in there, somewhere.

Moreover, to launch and run a successful professional service firm, the principals need to work even smarter every day, and with ever more energy. Talk about a formula for burnout! When I ask principals, "If you knew then what you know now, what would you do differently—for *yourself*, that is," many respond that they would really welcome more time to study, ponder, and create.

How would you go about cutting yourself some slack? Hugh Hochberg, principal consultant at The Coxe Group, discussed one way to avoid burnout. Hugh had worked with us on a forthright article that generated a lot of interest and admiration among editors, although it turned out to be too controversial for them to print. Its title was, "Sabbaticals Offer Multiple Benefits."

In Old Testament times, the sabbatical year came to an entire community every seven years, during which the land was to be fallow—a time of rejuvenation for the soil and of reconnection and reflection for the people. That's not what Hugh addressed, but it's interesting to see how old the concept is and from where the academic community got it.

In his article, Hugh salutes the firms that have set up sabbatical programs to reward an individual after much hard work and the corresponding success. The break—available to senior partners, minority partners, and nonowners alike—would enable the recipient to gain perspective and recharge.

When people go on sabbatical, the ones left behind benefit, too. They get a chance to grow into the vacated responsibilities. The firm realizes that it can survive the absence of a key individual. Well, why not? Walking in another person's shoes almost always breaks barriers to change and brings improvements.

Hugh even suggests that a sabbatical could be the start of a principal's transition to retirement; that is, the person who has been on sabbatical returns not to his prior responsibilities but rather to a more focused role. I am reminded of the architect who, during his semiretirement, took on the challenge of learning about and then setting up a design-build division for his firm. On his return, working just three days a week, he earned more for the firm and himself than in his previous six-day-a-week schedule.

What could bolster your knowledge and make you a better person and professional? Do you really know what it's like to run a hospital or provide physical therapy, if your clients are health-care institutions? What's really involved in teaching inner-city children, if you design or build schools?

I recall the story of another architect who got so frustrated with practicing the old-fashioned way, he set out—with his firm's blessing (and financing)—to discover what makes an American Main Street. After several months of travel around the U.S. and hundreds of interviews, he had the makings of a new thrust for his firm and new meaning in his life, not to mention insights that would benefit many towns.

Sabbaticals will certainly put relationships to the test. They represent "change" by another name. Key to this opportunity, therefore, is to assess how a time-out for certain valued people could benefit the entire firm.

There are books and online lists galore for faculty taking a sabbatical. For a professional services firm, here's some of what is entailed:

Define what could be achieved, and make the case.

Find the wherewithal to enable the separation.

Set the parameters for the person taking the sabbatical.

Communicate what will be expected as client and managerial responsibilities shift hands (whose?).

Monitor and support the countdown, so the departure is met with excitement, not disruptions.

Help the affected client team to understand the firm's initiative, and why you are temporarily providing a new project leader.

Supervise the shift of functions.

Welcome back the sabbatical-taker and reconstitute the firm as it was anticipated upon his or her return.

Make use of what the person has achieved on sabbatical, if it pertained to the firm. At the least, celebrate the achievement, which certainly will reflect well on everyone involved.

What really interests me about sabbaticals is not the program itself, but the *process* a firm follows once it has decided to initiate such a bold program. A sabbatical program creates an exceptional opportunity for a firm to clarify and communicate its values and how it operates. Firms get to discuss and then make long-awaited changes in their procedures and structure. "Transformation" or "reinvention" would not be overstating the effect.

PRINCIPLE 29

Anyone can become principled

I wrote this book to make it easier for principals and other members of the leadership of design and construction firms to guide their businesses. The first few times that I spoke about the importance and structure of business and marketing principles at professional conferences, I lectured, answered questions, and got the audience talking to each other about why and how they do things. Still, although they were getting good information, I wondered if they were really getting the hang of figuring out their own principles.

The opportunity to answer that question came at Build Boston 2003, when I challenged a panel of four industry and firm leaders—Gilbane's Alfred Potter, Shepley Bulfinch Richardson and Abbot's Malcolm Kent, SMMA's Michael Powers, and SWBR Architects' Thomas Zimmerman—to select and communicate the best of their own guiding principles. During the program, after each person presented his favorite principles, we broke up our large audience, mostly principals, into working groups that met with each of the panelists in sequence. I moved from circle to circle to assist everyone in discussing and crafting his or her own principles.

My message to the audience was that, far too often, people charged with leading firms or managing the work of others tend to explain *what* to do or *how*—when they should, instead, declare *why* they do something (or not). Knowing the reasons why a firm proceeds in a certain way, and having a snappy principle as a reminder, helps everyone to behave at peak effectiveness.

Here's how to forge your own principles:

Think of a situation or problem that you are facing. What's the issue? Has anything similar ever happened before? If yes, what solution succeeded in the past?

Consider what you might do to remedy the problem. Or learn what has succeeded in previous situations.

For each possible remedy, ask yourself why you would go that route instead of another. Keep going up the ladder until you reach the ultimate "because."

Convert that truth into a *brief* principle that will henceforth guide your own thoughts and actions.

Communicate the principle to others.

Here's how it works:

Problem: Getting project managers to understand how the *firm* makes money.

Remedy: Show them how we handle our money and where it goes.

Principle: **Design is a business.**

Tom Zimmerman, whose principle this is, also suggested, "Manage the money, not just the job" and "Open the books." He also leads by this principle: "If an employee is in trouble, it may be your fault."

Problem: Most people think that an outstanding proposal, followed by a great presentation, is what makes the client decide in their favor. Unfortunately, that's not always the case.

Remedies: Make sure that you are the client's preferred choice *before* the RFP is issued. Find out the *client's* value system.

Principle: **Don't trust your marketing to luck.**

Al Potter provided a string of principles for marketing, including "count the votes" and "presell the project." His principles give him the right to verify how well his people have gotten organized and done their homework before the proposal and also before the presentation. Another way he gets an early advantage is by following the principle to "share knowledge with your clients between projects. They are great business allies."

Problem: It's challenging enough to own a firm, but sometimes your people avoid the issues.

Remedies: Get everyone to share the firm's core values. Make sure that the principals are open and honest among themselves and with the staff. Be willing to part, if necessary.

Principle: **Take on the tough conversations.**

Mike Powers has a running start on devising principles and assessing their effectiveness because of SMMA's "Core Value System," which entails training and monitoring people's progress, as well as developing and committing to a personal mission statement.

Mike also contributed, "No question the staff asks is off limits!" and "Lead, don't manage." Obviously, being a good listener is key to his leadership style.

Problem: When the firm is large and the partnership diverse and busy, what can you do to keep quality and communication from drifting?

Remedy: Build close working and personal relationships with your colleagues, to transfer your firm's values, to reinforce your cohesiveness, and to enable you to trust others.

Principle: **None of us is as smart as all of us**—old Japanese proverb.

When the day of the Build Boston conference arrived, Carole Wedge, who was supposed to speak and who provided this axiom, had to be with her client in another state. Without missing a beat, her colleague Malcolm Kent stepped in, even using the handout Carole had prepared. "In our firm, we all believe that the client is paramount," Malcolm told the audience, voicing a principle that unifies SBRA and obviously enabled him to represent both Carole and the firm.

Later in the session, that statement about the client coming first created a dustup and provided an important lesson in principle-making. One of the people in the audience disagreed strongly. Her voice was raised, and discussion in that circle stalled while she vented her repudiation.

She posited that her guiding principle was "family comes first." I pointed out that principles are essentially neutral; the goal is to be true to your own principle. Therefore, I continued, she should surround herself with colleagues who similarly believe that the family is the first priority and extend to them the benefits and considerations implied in the principle. For her professional and personal life to be in equilibrium, it would probably also be wise for her clients to agree with her approach.

I have taken many audiences, clients, and my own staff through this exercise in devising principles. First, stating the problem forces people to confront what is not working for them—or what *is* working for them. Next, considering how various remedies would work in a variety of situations, and being open to seeing obstacles, clears a path for success.

Finally, coming up with a governing principle—and then using it to guide the work of others—is exceptionally satisfying. In fact, you will have learned something about yourself and your organization that will enable you to work more wisely and effectively in the future. That's fine preparation for leadership.

ABOUT THE AUTHOR

 Joan Capelin is a public relations master whose specialty is to build and protect the reputation of professional service providers, especially those in the design and construction industry. After working in-house for a variety of professional service firms, she founded Capelin Communications, Inc., a prominent public relations consulting firm, in 1981.

Her pioneering work and leadership in support of the professional services have earned her the Marketing Achievement Award from the Society for Marketing Professional Services (SMPS) as well as the rank of fellow and lifetime membership status. She was also accorded honorary membership in both the national and New York State component of The American Institute of Architects, the highest distinction the AIA gives to a non-architect.

Joan is highly regarded in the public relations community where she is accredited by the Public Relations Society of America (PRSA). She served as chair of the PRSA College of Fellows in 1999 and was the 2001 recipient of PRSA/New York's prestigious John W. Hill Award as that city's outstanding public relations professional. She is also the past president of Women Executives in Public Relations (WEPR).

An active speaker at conferences, corporations, and universities, Joan often writes articles and columns about professional services marketing, communications, and management. She has contributed to the SMPS Marketing Handbook for the Design & Construction Professional and edited 40 Effective Newsletters by A/E Firms.

Joan Capelin holds a B.A. from Wellesley College and an M.A. in French from Middlebury College. She is a Fulbright Scholar. Joan lives in New York City with her husband, David Paul Helpern, an architect.

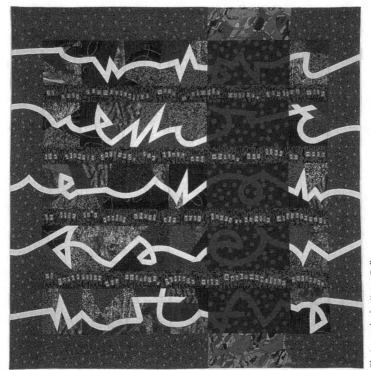

Cover art: "Read Between the Lines," a quilt of cotton fabrics by Robin Schwalb, 1995, 36"x36", inspired by the original haiku: "A flurry of words / puffs whitely into night air: / Read between the lines." The words appearing on this stitchery, portraying an interrupted conversation, are: "If only communication were a simple matter, dealing with the clearly defined, the black and white; but like so much in life it's really about the grey tones—subtle differences of perception and opinion, perhaps with Rashomon-like variety." The quilt is in Joan Capelin's collection of antique and contemporary folk art.

AVAILABLE FROM GREENWAY...

How Firms Succeed: A Field Guide to Design Management,
James P. Cramer and Scott Simpson.

A hands-on guide to running any design-related business—from a two-person graphics team to middle-management to CEOs of multi-national firms—offering advice on specific problems and situations and providing insight into the art of inspirational management and strategic thinking.

"*How Firms Succeed* is a fountainhead of great ideas for firms looking to not just survive, but thrive in today's challenging marketplace.
—Thompson E. Penney, FAIA
President/CEO, LS3P Architecture, Interior Architecture, Land Planning and President, The American Institute of Architects, 2003

Communication by Design, Joan Capelin

How to communicate—and, especially why—to clients, prospects, staff, and the public is the basis of this powerful book. It is targeted to business principals as well as anyone who aspires to a leadership position in a firm, association, or business joint venture.

"Joan Capelin offers thought-provoking practical lessons in marketing leadership—illustrated by interesting insights and implementable ideas. Read this book, put her advice into action, and your firm will flourish."
—Howard J. Wolff
Senior Vice President/Wimberly Allison Tong & Goo

Almanac of Architecture & Design, James P. Cramer and
Jennifer Evans Yankopolus, editors.

The only complete annual reference for rankings, records, and facts about architecture, interior design, landscape architecture, industrial design, and historic preservation.

"The reader who uses this book well will come away with a richer sense of the texture of the profession and of the architecture it produces."
—Paul Goldberger, The New Yorker

DesignIntelligence

The Design Futures Council's monthly "Report on the Future" provides access to key trends and issues on the cutting edge of the design professions. Each month it offers indispensable insight into management practices that will make any firm a better managed and more financially successful business.

"We read every issue with new enthusiasm because the information always proves so timely. No other publication in our industry provides as much useful strategy information."
—Davis Brody Bond LLP

—Order form on back—

ORDER FORM

How Firms Succeed: A Field Guide to Design Management: $39

Communication by Design: $34.95

Almanac of Architecture & Design: $49.50

***DesignIntelligence* (including a one-year membership to the Design Futures Council): $289 annually**

Shipping: $4.95
(add $1.50 per additional title)

NOTE: Shipping is included with *DesignIntelligence*—there is NO additional charge

Title	Quantity	Price:
	Shipping	
	Order Total	

❑ Check   ❑ Credit card

Card #   Expiration   Signature

Contact/Shipping Information

Name   Company

Address

City   State   Zip

Telephone   Fax

Email

Please fax this form to Greenway Communications: (770) 209-3778 or mail: Greenway Communications, 30 Technology Parkway South, Suite 200, Norcross, GA 30092. For additional information call (800) 726-8603.

östberg™

Library of Design Management

Every relationship of value requires constant care and commitment. At Östberg, we are relentless in our desire to create and bring forward only the best ideas in design, architecture, interiors, and design management. Using diverse mediums of communications, including books and the Internet, we are constantly searching for thoughtful ideas that are erudite, witty, and of lasting importance to the quality of life. Inspired by the architecture of Ragnar Östberg and the best of Scandinavian design and civility, the Östberg Library of Design Management seeks to restore the passion for creativity that makes better products, spaces, and communities. The essence of Östberg can be summed up in our quality charter to you: "Communicating concepts of leadership and design excellence."